OSPREY COMBAT AIRCRAFT • 47

F-15C/E EAGLE
UNITS OF OPERATION
IRAQI FREEDOM

SERIES EDITOR: TONY HOLMES

OSPREY COMBAT AIRCRAFT • 47

F-15C/E EAGLE UNITS OF OPERATION IRAQI FREEDOM

Steve Davies

OSPREY
PUBLISHING

Front cover
On 31 March 2003 the crew of
'Junker 68' – a 4th Fighter Wing (FW)
F-15E Strike Eagle – was tasked with
attacking targets in a kill box near
Baghdad city. Forced down to below
14,000 ft by poor weather, the crew
flew repeated passes over the target
area in a bid to locate Iraqi
Republican Guard vehicles, of which
there was said to be many. But on
the third and final pass all hell broke
loose, as pilot, 'Hacker' relates;

'We were already climbing up to
conserve fuel on the way home, and
I had barely finished my turn when
the RWR (Radar Warning Receiver)
screamed its stuttering wail in my
headset. The noise chilled me to the
bone – it was the missile launch
tone. Before I looked at the RWR
itself, my eyes cued in on the blaz-
ingly bright red warning light on the
instrument panel, located just below
the glareshield at eye level. It is only
the size of a dime, but the black
words backlit on the square red light
jumped out at me larger than life –
"SAM". At the same time my WSO
(Weapons System Operator),
"Maddog", shouted "ROLAND!".'

'Junker 68' had become the target
for two French-built Roland surface-
to-air missiles (SAMs), ripple-fired
one after the other. The discharging
of chaff by 'Hacker', combined with
sustained high-g SAM-defeating
manoeuvring, allowed the Strike
Eagle crew to make good their
escape. Both missiles had been
tracking the F-15E, and 'Hacker' and
'Maddog' were fully aware that their
chances of surviving two Roland
launches whilst in the heart of the
missiles' engagement envelope had
been slim indeed. This, and other
such close encounters with death,
served as a stark reminder to the
crews of the 4th FW that the Iraqi
Republican Guard were more than
capable of fighting back when the
conditions were right (*Cover artwork
by Mark Postlethwaite*)

This book is dedicated to the memory of Maj Bill 'Salty' Watkins III and Capt
Eric 'Boot' Das

First published in Great Britain in 2004 by Osprey Publishing
Elms Court, Chapel Way, Botley, Oxford, OX2 9LP

ISBN 1 84176 802 2

Edited by Tony Holmes and Bruce Hales-Dutton
Page design by Tony Truscott
Cover Artwork by Mark Postlethwaite
Aircraft Profiles by Chris Davey
Scale Drawings by Mark Styling
Index by Alan Thatcher
Origination by Grasmere Digital Imaging, Leeds, UK
Printed in China through Bookbuilders

04 05 06 07 08   10 9 8 7 6 5 4 3 2 1

ACKNOWLEDGEMENTS
The Author would like to thank all those who helped him research and write this
book. Particular thanks go to Brig Gen Eric J Rosborg and all at the 4th FW. Special
thanks go to Lt Cols Daryl Roberson, Mark Kelly, Gary Klett and Doug Reynolds,
Maj Jolly Ronald, Sqn Ldr Steve Formoso, Capts Drew Whiat, Joe Siberski, David
Small, Randall Haskin, Greg Craven, John Bremer, Bob Bryant, James Weir, Nikki
Das, Rich Meziere, Christian Burbach and Jeff Jones, 1Lts Kimberly Turner and Gary
Marlowe and 2Lt Jamie Humphreys and Tom Murphy.

The USAF was immensely supportive of this book, with Brig Gen Rosborg in
particular being a staunch supporter of the endeavour to write an accurate and truthful
account of the 4th FW's contribution to the war in Iraq. Despite this, some areas of
my research were too sensitive for the USAF to provide official comment on.
Therefore, in order to write such a complete overview of the Strike Eagle's
contribution to the war effort, I have also had to rely on non-attributable interviews
conducted with individuals without the official sanction of the USAF.

EDITOR'S NOTE
To make this best-selling series as authoritative as possible, the Editor would be
interested in hearing from any individual who may have relevant photographs,
documentation or first-hand experiences relating to the world's elite pilots, and their
aircraft, of the various theatres of war. Any material used will be credited to its original
source. Please contact Tony Holmes via e-mail at:
tony.holmes@osprey-jets.freeserve.co.uk

CONTENTS

EAGLE GENEALOGY

Based on the McDonnell Douglas 199-B design, the F-15A Eagle prototype first rolled out of the company's St Louis, Missouri, plant on 26 June 1972. The jet made its first flight on 27 July and production examples entered service with the 1st TFW at Langley AFB, Virginia, in January 1976. Since then, the aircraft has matured into the world's most successful fighter, becoming the interceptor of choice over the skies of Iraq since the 1991 Gulf War.

The keys to the Eagle's superiority are its superb radar, excellent supporting avionics and reliable, maintenance-friendly airframe. It boasts a very simple, fixed-geometry, cambered wing design, characterised by smooth lines and a distinct absence of high lift devices. This wing was optimised for high-subsonic manoeuvrability, and conferred a 21.5-degree per second sustained turn rate, as well as superb instantaneous turn rate, for an enhanced air combat manoeuvring experience.

'McAir' implemented a revolutionary concept that complimented the radar and weapons systems – HOTAS. Hands On Throttle And Stick was a euphemism for the science of placing switches and buttons within easy reach of the pilot's thumbs and fingers, which was accomplished by locating them strategically on the throttle and control stick grip. Such ingenuity has enabled F-15 pilots to score kills in scenarios when they might otherwise have been too busy 'heads down', locating a switch or setting up a series of switches or perfuming some other labour-intensive task.

HOTAS was complimented by a head-up display (HUD) that employed two combining glasses on to which a wide range of flight and weapons system information was projected. It too increased the pilot's awareness by allowing him to keep his eyes outside the aircraft for longer.

The F-15C Eagle is the world's premier interceptor, this example hailing from the RAF Lakenheath-based 493rd FS/48th FW. An ex-33rd TFW machine, this jet has served with the USAFE-controlled 48th FW since March 1994 *(author/FJ Photography.com)*

McDonnell Douglas refined the Eagle design in the form of the F-15C, which featured an increased combat radius. First flown on 26 February 1979, the C-model was visually indistinguishable from the F-15A apart from having a new ACES II ejection seat and subtle improvements to the landing gear to cater for its heavier take-off weight. The jet also featured a full avionics fit, with a comprehensive Tactical Electronic Warfare System (TEWS) which had been absent from most A-models, an additional (UHF) radio and strengthened airframe

components. The two-seat F-15D was identical to the C-model except for the deleted AN/ALQ-135(V) ICMS (Internal CounterMeasures Set) jammer line replaceable units, which had been displaced from the avionics bay behind the pilot in the C-model by the second cockpit.

February 1983 saw the introduction of additional modifications to the F-15C fleet when Multiple Stage Improvement Program II (MSIP II) was introduced to F-15C/Ds rolling off the production line and then retrofitted to the entire F-15 inventory, including A/B-models. The first fully-upgraded MSIP-II F-15C (84-0001) was flown in June 1985.

MSIP-II created a 25 per cent increase in systems reliability, and saw the installation of the Hughes AN/APG-70 radar (an advanced radar derived from the APG-63), a faster central computer with more memory, a new multi-purpose colour display to replace an the existing analogue armament panel, wiring and software to integrate JTIDS (joint tactical information distribution system, which was installed in very limited numbers, and was replaced by Fighter Data Link in 2001), new throttles, a video tape recording system that recorded the HUD and radar for post-flight debriefing and kill validation, improvements to the aircraft's electronic warfare system and support for the AIM-120 AMRAAM (Advanced Medium Range Air-to-Air Missile). The APG-70 was used for a short time only, however, as it was superseded by the updated APG-63(V)I. HOTAS was fully refined following the implementation of MSIP, which integrated a new throttle design and a stick grip with a greater array of buttons.

HOTAS was a revolutionary concept which drastically enhanced the way the pilot interfaced with, and operated, the Eagle's weapons system and avionics. By carefully positioning a host of switches and buttons on the stick and throttles, it was possible for the pilot to intuitively exploit the jet's complex systems when in flight (*author/FJ Photography.com*)

The AN/APG-63(V)0, (V)1 and (V)2 and AN/APG-70 radars have been the key to the F-15C's long-range interception capabilities. Subjected to constant updates and upgrades, they have provided the fighter with unparalleled Beyond Visual Range capabilities (*author/FJ Photography.com*)

APG-63 RADAR

The F-15's radar was built by Hughes following a parallel tender process similar to the Eagle's F-X or Fighter Experimental programme that had seen the jet selected for

USAF service as a replacement for the F-4 Phantom II. The radar is the F-15's single most important asset, and Hughes was awarded the tender in 1968 on the premise that it would produce an advanced system with an all-weather capability against airborne threats (including AIM-7 Sparrow missile guidance provisions and 'look-down, shoot-down' capability) and provisions for cueing optical tracking systems that might appear on the jet at a later date, as seen on the air-to-ground F-15E. Additionally, a limited capability against ground threats was also incorporated.

The $82m contract, awarded in October 1970, eventually yielded the APG-63 radar. It could track targets in ground clutter using Doppler shift and employed high and medium pulse repetition frequencies (PRFs) to track targets at different ranges, altitudes, aspects and closing speeds according to pre-programmed modes selected by the pilot. The radar could also interrogate a contact with identification friend or foe (IFF) to determine if it was a 'friendly'. In the ground mode it could map the terrain ahead and update the inertial navigation system (INS), as well as providing steering cues in order to successfully bomb a ground target – F-15A/B/C/D variants were capable of carrying and employing a wide range of air-to-ground weaponry, although this capability was officially deleted by the USAF following the service introduction of the F-15E.

In summary, the APG-63 radar represented a quantum leap beyond existing capabilities, and while being tailored for ease of use, it simultaneously provided maximum situational awareness for the pilot.

The F-15C has used several different radars – APG-63(V)0, APG-70, APG-63(V)I and APG-63(V)2 – and all but the last are closely based on the original APG-63 design. Each took advantage of advances in computing and technology as they occurred, and each, therefore, has its own nuances. However, they could all be characterised as utilising medium, high and interleaved PRFs, ground moving target rejection algorithms to reject false ground returns and a core base of main- and sub-operating modes selected according to a range of tactical and environmental factors.

The main search mode was interleaved mode (range while search), which provided a good compromise between scan volume, detection range and data generation in order to allow long-range air-to-air surveillance. It was also reasonably jam-resistant.

F-15E STRIKE EAGLE

The F-15E Strike Eagle was the dedicated multi-role adaptation of the original Eagle airframe, and was unquestionably the most capable, well-rounded, strike fighter yet built. McDonnell Douglas and Hughes had recognised that the USAF might well be interested in a two-seat, dedicated strike version of the F-15 and set about developing this concept under the internal project name 'Strike Eagle'. The

Family tree. The Strike Eagle's roots are plain, its heritage second to none (*Boeing via author*)

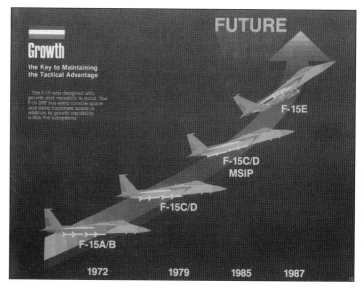

The F-111F had a fearsome reputation as an airframe that could go very low, very fast and for a long, long way. Despite the F-15E's inability to match the mighty 'Vark' statistically, its self-protection capabilities, newer avionics and weapons systems, superb synthetic aperture radar and dramatically enhanced survivability have made it a worthy successor. This example, serving with the 494th TFS/48th TFW, is seen dropping ballute-retarded Mk 82 AIR 500-lb bombs over a range at Nellis AFB during a *Red Flag* exercise in the late 1980s. A veteran of Operation *Desert Storm*, this jet (72-1443) was replaced by an F-15E at RAF Lakenheath in 1992. It was then used by the 524th FS/27th FW at Cannon AFB, New Mexico, until retired to the Aerospace Maintenance & Regeneration Center at Davis-Monthan AFB, Arizona, on 16 July 1996 (*USAF*)

consortium received positive encouragement from Tactical Air Command (TAC) boss Gen Wilbur Creech, who was worried that as his F-111 fleet grew older, TAC would lose its edge in the deep strike role. This crucial mission in Western Europe was fulfilled by 70+ F-111Es and Fs divided into two wings at RAF Upper Heyford and RAF Lakenheath.

Savaged by the world's media in its early years, the F-111 had matured into a potent strike platform which offered long range, terrain following and precision strike capabilities. Its Pave Tack pod used infra-red imaging to allow the crew to visually acquire targets at night. The system could also direct a laser onto the target to allow the employment of laser-guided bombs (LGBs) to home in on the reflected energy and strike the target with pinpoint accuracy. Finally, the F-111's terrain following radar (TFR) would allow the crew to fly down to 200 ft above ground level in all weathers, thereby avoiding enemy radar and visual detection. With all this mission capability, the F-111 would be a hard act to follow.

APG-70 AIR-TO-GROUND RADAR

Hughes went back to the drawing board to completely overhaul and improve the APG-63 for the Strike Eagle. The result was the APG-70, complete with synthetic aperture radar. SAR, which was deleted in the version of APG-70 fitted into the F-15C, measured the Doppler shift created when radar waves hit the ground and bounced back to the antenna. Using complex computer algorithms to establish the movement of the aircraft relative to the ground, the APG-70 interpreted these shifts and translated them into a top-down picture in the two-place cockpit. The resulting image gave a very clear view of the ground, which, when viewed by the pilot or WSO, looked very similar to a bird's eye view of the target area. This process became known as 'patch mapping', and could be achieved down to a resolution of 0.67 of a nautical mile.

Two other key components were integrated into the Strike Eagle – LANTIRN (Low Altitude Navigation Targeting Infra Red for Night) and conformal fuel tanks (CFTs). The latter, sitting flush along the aircraft's fuselage below the wing root, also featured weapons hard points to allow additional stores to be carried. The LANTIRN system, built by Martin Marietta for the USAF, combined forward looking infra-red optics and TFR. Housed in two pods, the LANTIRN equipment would eventually be mounted below the engine nacelles.

Achieving operational status in 1987, the AAQ-13 navigation pod and AAQ-14 targeting pod (TP), were each attached to the F-15E via two mounted lugs and simple electrical terminals. The 'nav pod' housed a FLIR sensor and TFR, and was primarily used by the pilot to allow hands-off low altitude flying in all weathers, night or day. The FLIR sensor looked ahead of the aircraft and could display the resulting image onto the pilot's Kaiser Wide Field of View (WFOV) HUD. The TFR looked ahead and slightly to either side of the aircraft to detect obstacles and terrain.

Mounted on the left pylon was the TP. Used by the WSO to identify and designate targets when weather conditions permitted, it could be tied to the radar or manipulated independently. It had three selectable fields of view and housed a laser designator with which to guide LGBs to the target. The WSO had to find his target in the TP, put the cross hairs over it and press a button to commit the pod to tracking it. Several tracking options were available, all of which permitted the WSO to keep one eye on other systems during the course of the attack run – something that F-111F WSOs were never able to do.

The F-15E was also modified to allow a 16,000-hour fatigue life. The jet's forward avionics bays were redesigned (along with changes to the electrical system which powered them) and the ammunition carriage space for the M61A1 Vulcan cannon was reduced in size to make way for additional avionics. The engine bays were redesigned to allow commonality in plumbing and installation of either Pratt & Whitney or General Electric engines, and the tail hook was modified to accommodate a heavier anticipated landing weight. These modifications permitted a new sustained 9G capability, but dictated the installation of a new landing

Left and below
LANTIRN afforded the F-15E pilot and WSO a host of functions to improve the safety of low-level penetrations at night and in bad weather. The NAVFLIR in the HUD turned pitch black into a monochrome green and allowed visual acquisition of obstacles ahead. The target pod had a lower resolution than that of the F-111 but was easier to use and manipulate, and offered the WSO the option of several different tracking modes (*Author/FJ Photography.com*)

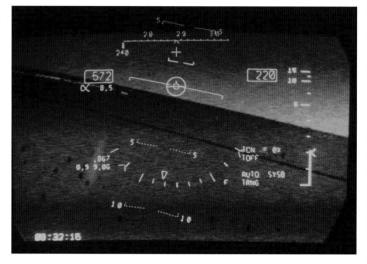

As this McDonnell Douglas-produced graphic clearly shows, the Strike Eagle was designed to operate autonomously, making full use of its air-to-air and air-to-ground capabilities (*Boeing via Author*)

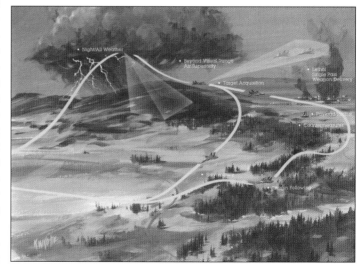

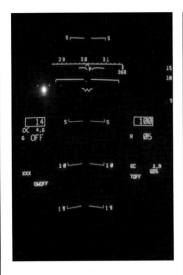

The WFOV HUD (above), large-format MPDs (above right) and UFC (right) are key components of the Strike Eagle's cockpit interoperability. Combined, they confer an extension to the HOTAS system, giving both crewmembers full control over the jet's complex systems, often at the touch of a single button (*Author/FJ Photography.com*)

gear to permit safe operations at higher gross weight. In all, the F-15E weighed in some 16,000 lbs heavier than the F-15C, with a maximum take-off weight of 81,000 lbs.

Internally, the two-place cockpit was considerably updated. There was an emphasis on interoperability so that each crew member could perform almost any function needed to complete the mission. The front cockpit featured two monochrome multi purpose displays (MPD) and one colour MPD (MPCD). The rear cockpit housed two MPDs and two MPCDs. An UFC (up front controller) was also installed in each cockpit to allow the crew to enter data into the sophisticated avionics suite.

The USAF ordered the F-15E in 1984 following a six-month competition against the General Dynamics F-16XL. July 1985 saw the first F-15E (86-0183) make its maiden flight, and in August of the following year the 33rd TFW at Eglin AFB, in Florida, began USAF acceptance trials with the jet after receiving three Strike Eagles. Finally, in December 1988, the F-4E-equipped 4th TFW at Seymour Johnson AFB, in North Carolina, became the first USAF wing to commence transition onto the F-15E. To date, 230 Strike Eagles have been built for the USAF.

WATCHFUL EYES

For over a decade, Coalition forces patrolled the southern no-fly zone below the 32nd Parallel and the northern no-fly zone above the 36th Parallel in an attempt to contain Iraqi dictator Saddam Hussein. Those units charged with enforcing the containment of Iraqi aircraft, helicopters and military vehicles – termed Operation *Southern Watch* (OSW) and Operation *Northern Watch* (ONW) – came from the UK and the US, with France contributing forces until the mid-1990s. Both operations matured from a sketchy and somewhat ill-conceived cease-fire arrangement negotiated with Iraq by the US at the end of the Gulf War in 1991 to highly effective US-led barriers that protected Iraq's impoverished Shiites in the south and Kurds to the north.

Banking away from the camera to reveal a mixed air-to-air and air-to-ground load of two GBU-12s, two AIM-120 AMRAAM, two AIM-9M Sidewinder and two AIM-7M Sparrow missiles, this Lakenheath-based Strike Eagle patrols the southern no-fly zone in late 1998 (*Gary Klett via author*)

PREPARATIONS

From 1998 onwards, F-15Cs deployed to both operations under the Aerospace Expeditionary Forces (AEF) concept. This represented the road map which defined the units to be deployed to particular locations some 15 months before they actually left their home bases. Previously, deployments had been according to a haphazard system which allowed little forward-planning and was completely unreliable. It was not unheard of for an Eagle unit to deploy for what it understood to be a 40-day stint, only to end up staying for over 70. AEF, by contrast, committed a unit for a 90-day deployment, making it likely that the unit would return home on the prescribed date, give or take a few days. AEF had completed three full cycles by the time Operation *Iraqi Freedom* (OIF) superseded OSW and ONW in April 2003.

Prince Sultan Air Base ('PSAB'), in Saudi Arabia, most frequently hosted F-15C deployments to OSW, while Incirlik AB, in Turkey, provided the temporary home for F-15 squadrons deploying to ONW. Prior to leaving on any AEF, or pre-planned, operation, it was customary for the squadron to work-up and intensify training so that essential skills could be honed. Capt Nick Guttmann, who has two OSW deployments to his credit, 1000 hours in the Eagle and is a graduate of the F-15 Fighter Weapons School, commented;

'We would change the focus of the squadron to start practising the no-fly mission, which brings some particular differences into play. It's a defensive mindset where you don't have the initiative. You have a presence, but all the cards are with the adversary. They decide what happens and you have to be ready for anything. That brings its own challenges. It's also something of an anomaly because you're in hostile territory doing a defensive mission, which at first seems odd. You're simultaneously defending against an air threat – trying to keep them behind an imaginary line – yet the surface threat is right beneath you, shooting at you the whole time. It's challenging.'

Even so, there was significant apathy towards OSW and ONW as time wore on, and by the late 1990s a nonchalance had crept into the USAF that contrasted strikingly with the situation in OSW's formative years. Squadrons next on the schedule would telephone around other fighter units to arrange dissimilar air combat training, or book airspace and training range time to prepare their pilots. Whereas they would have received priority treatment in OSW's earlier years, by 2001 a deployment to 'PSAB' or Incirlik created few ripples. Indeed, a unit could expect a diminished degree of special treatment, if any at all. This was particularly true for those squadrons based in Europe, where airspace issues with host nations compounded the problem.

Faced with such difficulties, units turned to 'in-squadron training' – a euphemism for sending an eight-ship flight of F-15s up so that four could practice no-fly zone defence whilst the others played the adversary ('Red Air') – as the training tool of choice. According to Guttmann;

'In-squadron was really about making the best of a bad situation. It was really only of use to four pilots, because the guys flying "Red Air" were focusing exclusively on delivering an accurate replication of the threat. So four pilots got training and four did not. What we really wanted was good airspace and good support from other fighter wings, where we could have made a verbal agreement with other squadrons to help them get ready when it was their turn to deploy.'

A 493rd FS pilot completes last minute paperwork pertaining to the mechanical state of his F-15C before climbing the ladder and strapping in to conduct one last CT sortie from RAF Lakenheath prior to embarking on another OSW deployment. It was essential to train as hard as possible before arrival in Saudi Arabia. Once there, the quality of training was so poor that key skills would soon degrade
(*author/FJ Photography.com*)

In the run-up to a deployment to Turkey, Saudi Arabia or Kuwait (several other countries supported OSW deployments, including Bahrain, Qatar and Oman), some of the basics were again stressed to junior and experienced pilots alike. These included communications procedures, fuel management and lost wingman procedures. Such priceless combat environment skills are taught at the start of a pilot's training, but they can decay if not practiced incessantly.

PRINCE SULTAN AIR BASE

Pentagon and Central Command planners dictated the number of squadron airframes and pilots assigned to each deployment. A 'pilot ratio' was derived by calculating the number of aircrew required for deployment on a 24-hour-a-day, seven-days-a-week basis. An entire squadron of 18 aircraft was usually deployed, although the size was dictated by the overall balance of other Coalition assets in the region. For example, when the 493rd FS deployed in 2001, it was the only air superiority squadron in-theatre, and therefore committed all 18 of its F-15Cs. But when the 71st FS/1st FW deployed later that year it brought with it only 12 F-15Cs because an F-16 squadron was already assigned to aerial defence duties.

The heart and brains of OSW's air operations was the Combined Air Operations Centre (CAOC), which moved in 2001 from military quarters in Riyadh to Prince Sultan Air Base, thus centralising the entire OSW mission planning element. The CAOC generated a daily Air Tasking Order (ATO) for all Coalition OSW participants (including naval and other aviation assets aboard aircraft carriers in the Northern Arabian Gulf or on land at bases in Kuwait, Oman and other neighbouring countries) and was staffed by a representative of each airframe and each air force in-theatre. The F-15 CAOC representative worked exclusively between 90 and 120 days whilst assigned to the centre, and he was usually a Fighter Weapons School graduate, known colloquially as a 'patch wearer'. Capt Guttmann recounted;

'Because the missions were very similar each day, and because the communication between the CAOC and the squadrons was so good during the last few years of OSW, we could typically get a rough outline of the "frag" (ATO) about three days ahead of time. That's never going to happen in an actual shooting war, when you'd be lucky to get the information 12 hours before, but it's how OSW worked. As each day passed, we'd get more information to the point that, 24 hours ahead of time, we had a detailed plan not just of what we were doing, but also of what everyone else was doing. They ran three ATOs at the same time – Day 1, Day 2 and Day 3. By the time Day 1's ATO was executed, the people working on it would start planning Day 4, so it was just a revolving process.'

In basic terms, OSW and ONW tasked the F-15C with pursuing Iraqi aircraft violating the no-fly zone whilst simultaneously protecting all other friendly aircraft in-theatre, including tankers, reconnaissance aircraft, AWACS, J-STARS and helicopters. Guttman explained;

'It's about maintaining the status quo. We didn't want anything changing. It's a show of force, a presence mission. We would take about six jets for a given mission and man the skies for that piece of real-estate for a vulnerability time. That time could be three hours of one day and five of the next, depending upon what the generals in charge wanted. That

The Coalition liked to work at night whenever possible, for it was in the hours of darkness that they enjoyed the additional advantage of being virtually invisible to Iraqi AAA gunners, who could literally not see them. Coalition investment in night vision devices, and the inherent night capabilities of aircraft like the Strike Eagle, tipped the scales even further in the allies' favour (*Gary Klett via author*)

mission could change if the U-2 was being flown over Baghdad, which required more assets to achieve. That mission would see the reconnaissance jet airborne for a long time, which meant that we would have to be up for a long time too. It was therefore easier to schedule our refuelling if we took ten jets and spaced them out, instead of taking six and stretching things. They were long missions. We'd sit in the cockpit for about 10.5 hours, with 8.5 of that being on station. The squadron would fly two of these missions a day.

'When the U-2 wasn't flying, missions were significantly shorter, and the squadron would usually fly only one mission per day. Had we changed from maintaining the status quo to an actual shooting war, we would have operated something like 12 jets at the same time, depending on the air threat that we had expected to see.'

To execute the ATO for 24 hours a day, each F-15C squadron supplied enough mission commander-qualified pilots to guarantee that at least one was available at any time. The mission commander (MC) was a highly-experienced Coalition pilot who was able to run the ATO from the moment the mission was briefed to the time it landed and debriefed. That meant anything from making changes to the plan due to any unforeseen pop-up threat to reacting to rapidly changing weather conditions – whatever the situation dictated. The MC was not always an F-15C pilot, as the ATO alternated between airframes on a daily basis, but the unit still had to ensure that one was always available for contingency purposes.

SORTIES AND THREATS

Once airborne and 'on station' (pilot parlance for being over enemy territory at the CAP location and ready to go to work), the Eagles would split into two-aircraft elements. Four-ship flights were always tactically preferable and easier to justify over the smaller expanse of territory policed by ONW. On the other hand, the knowledge that the Iraqi Air Force (IrAF) was largely predictable, with an undetected *en masse* attack highly unlikely, plus the huge expanse of real estate policed by OSW, resulted in the Eagles spreading their picketing envelope.

With Iraq's major military airfields always under radar surveillance, it was therefore impossible for a single aircraft to be launched without the

Coalition immediately knowing about it. If a large force of Iraqi aircraft was detected, there was ample time to call upon additional F-15s to provide support if required.

The IrAF adopted a predominantly non-confrontational stance for much of ONW and OSW, preferring to conduct training missions within the confines of airspace outside the no-fly zones. It was not always so subservient, however. When launched into action, the IrAF used feints and ruses to try and lure Coalition jets into traps, or to expose high-value assets like tankers and AWACS aircraft to attack. The most infamous of these ruses was the 'high fast flyer' – a MiG-25 'Foxbat' which flew into the no-fly zone at Mach 2.5 and headed directly for a high-value asset. This created several problems, for the Eagles had to react quickly if they were to protect their charges, thus exposing gaps in the CAP screen.

The theory was that the 'Foxbat' drew the cover away by attracting its attention, thus allowing other IrAF fighters to mount slashing attacks on the unprotected aircraft. The technique was at least predicable, if not easy to counter because of the high speeds involved. The F-15 was the only Coalition fighter with both the internal fuel and engagement capability to deal with it.

Most missions drew a certain amount of ground fire from AAA or SAM operators, who actively engaged Coalition jets in direct contravention of the 1991 cease-fire agreement. While most AAA is ineffective below 15,000 ft, the upper end of the AAA calibre scale – 100 mm – posed a risk even at the medium altitudes at which the Eagles 'perched'. This unguided, barrage fire could be dodged, and was largely fired to harass. But accurate fire could easily have brought an F-15 down, so it was regarded with respect. SAM launches were less prolific than AAA fire, but they represented the most serious threat because wily operators soon learned to launch their missiles with visual, rather than radar, guidance. This denied pilots electronic indications of a launch and made it very difficult to locate a SAM in flight.

Another interesting tactic used by Iraqi pilots saw ground- and air-based threats combined to form a 'honey trap'. MiG pilots would attempt to lure Eagles from their CAP stations into the engagement envelopes of previously unknown SAM rings or AAA gun engagement zones (GEZ). Sometimes they were successful. The tactic was often initiated by the MiG breaking through the no-fly zone and then running as soon as the F-15 CAP was committed to intercept. The pursuing Eagles then got a face full of lead or came under SAM fire. It was quickly established that Eagle drivers should be wary of giving chase to a MiG heading in a direction other than its home air base. Capt Guttman experienced just such an incident;

'On my 23rd mission I led my wingman to investigate an AWACS track of interest. AWACS believed it was a MiG-29 on a test flight inside

This Egyptian SA-2 SAM site was photographed from the back seat of an F-15E during an exercise with the Egyptian Air Force. Iraqi SA-2 and SA-3 sites similar in appearance to this one dotted the landscape north and south of the no-fly zones (*Gary Klett via author*)

sovereign Iraqi airspace. We knew they that occasionally flew their "Fulcrums", and we wanted to get a better idea of how many they were operating. We were despatched to take a look and, upon committing to the track (leaving the CAP station to investigate), the MiG promptly returned to base. As we came within range, we were illuminated and engaged by SA-2 and SA-3 missile sites. I ordered combat jettison of wing tanks as we evaded the threat and the engagement came to nothing. We turned tail and returned to our CAP station. It was only after we landed that I had the opportunity to explain to my wingman, who was flying his first combat mission, that OSW missions were rarely that exciting!'

COMMAND, CONTROL & COMMUNICATIONS

Acting as a communications relay between the CAOC and the mission commander, the E-3 AWACS was the key to the successful execution of each ATO. Its importance in this role increased with the introduction of a pre-planned retaliatory strike framework that allowed what became known as response options (ROs). No-fly zone enforcers could react to threats or incursions in a coordinated manner by executing agreed ROs against pre-determined targets.

The Eagles worked most closely with the SEAD (Suppression of Enemy Air Defences) escorts whose job it was to protect the package from surface threats. This was made easier once in flight by using AWACS to coordinate the other package elements, leaving the F-15 flight leader to talk to the F-16CJs, F/A-18s or EA-6Bs. Knowing the day's ROs simplified the job of protecting the strike force, enabling the F-15Cs to operate with fluidity when the CAOC spontaneously executed one. Once the Eagles and SEAD assets were on station, the strike aircraft were free to roam the airspace inside the no-fly zone to investigate targets of interest, and to engage in simulated weapons releases and attacks.

'Safe' routes allowed aircraft with battle damage or malfunctioning IFF equipment to fly within the confines of prescribed corridors to avoid being shot down. Aircraft detected in these corridors were visually intercepted and identified by a pair of Eagles as soon as possible.

It was straightforward for both the F-15C and the AWACS to identify intruders long before they breached the no-fly zone, although low-altitude contacts sometimes threw up false alarms. On one particular occasion Capt Guttman recalled how an inexperienced AWACS controller had called 'bandits inbound' at 'low-altitude and close range', precipitating a frantic intercept by the F-15s assigned to protect the high-value asset. The Eagle pilots reported no bogies in sight, or on radar, and it was later established that the AWACS radar had 'guessed' the position of an Iraqi fighter whose track it had lost. The IrAF jet had actually landed, but the radar's logic had continued to plot the 'estimated path' of the contact – over the no-fly zone and straight at the E-3 at low level. The controller had failed to recognise the situation, causing a few hearts to beat faster.

MAINTAINING CURRENCY

For the pilots deployed to Saudi Arabia there were critical issues in maintaining currency. With fewer sorties flown during a 90-day OSW deployment than in a similar peace-time domestic scenario, the unavoidable reality was that missions flown over southern Iraq were usually uneventful and did not always contribute to maintaining pilot proficiency. Each squadron was therefore responsible for planning and executing its own continuation training (CT) sorties when not flying in support of the ATO. However, a fickle Saudi government dictated the number of CT sorties allowed from 'PSAB', reflecting the nature of relations with the US at any given time. Consequently, pilots rarely flew sorties outside the ATO.

Capt Guttman spent 70 days at 'PSAB' in 1998 and flew a meagre 21 combat missions (defined as missions over the Iraqi border and into the no-fly zone) in that time. He later accumulated just nine more combat missions in the eight weeks of a subsequent 2001 OSW deployment. From the moment the Eagle pilots arrived in-theatre there was a steady deterioration of their combat skills until the day they left. Guttman summarised it;

'Our ability to do CT was turned on or turned off by the Saudi government, and it was extremely detrimental to our ability to do the job. You got fairly good at dodging AAA, but you became progressively worse at just about everything else. There weren't even any simulators there to practice with. It's been said for years that combat is five per cent adrenalin and 95 per cent boredom, and you have to be ready when it happens. You're only going to get one shot at it, and you've got to get it right. The skills of the squadron's pilots came down so significantly that when we got back home we started again from scratch. We took the external tanks off of the jet and started with the basics – taking two clean jets to do one-versus-one dogfighting until we remembered how to do that. Then we went two-versus-one, then two-versus-two. Sixty days later we went back to what we were doing before we left – eight-versus-eight.'

The F-15C had battered the IrAF during Operation *Desert Storm* in 1991. And although the Eagle had not bloodied its claws over Iraq since then, many of the aircraft used to score kills were still policing the no-fly zones some 12 years later. These two F-15Cs are credited with downing two Iraqi fighters apiece, and at the time of writing were in the inventory of the 493rd FS/48th FW at RAF Lakenheath (*author/FJ Photography.com*)

ROs AND THE F-15E

The F-15E Strike Eagle was the primary tool for enforcing and implementing Response Options and making spontaneous retaliatory strikes over Iraq prior to OIF. During the early 1990s the jet had been used to neutralise many of the threatening SAM and AAA systems which often took pot shots at loitering Coalition aircraft. But in the years leading up to the second Gulf War, a pre-planned, RO-oriented modus operandi became the norm.

The F-15E wings were the most highly-tasked of any tactical fighter operators within the USAF because there were fewer Strike Eagle squadrons to fulfil AEF missions. Of the six operational F-15E units, three were also assigned to the emergency air expeditionary wing (AEW) concept – the 335th and 336th FSs of the 4th AEW and the 391st FS of the 366th AEW. The 90th FS/3rd FW was assigned to Pacific Air Force duties, and was therefore exempt from AEF cycles until 2002. The 48th FW's two F-15E squadrons – the 492nd and 494th FSs – carried the dual responsibility of assignment not only to USAF Europe but also to NATO.

The road to adopting ROs as the primary means of enforcing the OSW/ONW mission passed several different stages. Initially, immediate responses to AAA or SAM launches were replaced with delayed, punitive strikes, often flown the same day, but adhering to the adage that 'retaliation is a dish best eaten cold'. This soon evolved into an even more considered approach, whereby the Coalition exercised the right to attack *any* Iraqi military target in the southern no-fly zone. It did not even have to be the one that prompted the reaction in the first place. This, in turn, led to the adoption of the pre-planned RO methodology. Capt Randall Haskin, a 336th FS Strike Eagle pilot, explained;

'This philosophy was basically that it was better to come back later with all of the appropriate assets on hand than it was to knee-jerk react to getting shot at and risk actually getting hit.'

ROs offered real advantages in terms of safety, precision, reduction in the possibility of collateral damage and achieving the job with minimum firepower. Each Strike Eagle crew planned and prepared to attack its targets as it would on any other mission. If the CAOC called for an RO to be executed while the package was in flight, there was an excellent chance that the target would be struck with precision and good effect. According to one F-15E pilot, the nature of these marauding strike packages led the Strike Eagle community to coin the phrase 'roving motor cycle gang'. He added, 'We were like a group of bikers loaded with weapons looking for a fight and going no place in particular'.

The CAOC could raise an ATO which called specifically for a measured response to increasing Iraqi violations or a particularly serious misdemeanour. In such cases the crew briefed for both primary and secondary targets, before launching in exactly the same way they would for a routine OSW patrol. It was just that they knew as they headed out of the door and stepped towards the waiting aircraft that this time they would definitely be dropping 'iron'.

The Strike Eagle flew three main types of OSW sortie: 'containers', which involved penetrating the no-fly zone as strikers or defensive counter air fighters scouting for Iraqi aircraft; alerts, where crews waited for the 'bat 'phone' to ring and scramble them to investigate a target in the no-fly zone; and normal CTs, which allowed air-to-air practice.

F-15E OSW deployments were always made to either Al Jaber AB, in Kuwait, or Sheikh Isa AB, in Bahrain, as well as Al Udeid AB, in Qatar, for OIF, because of the political implications of having strikers based in Saudi Arabia. Crews therefore had numerous opportunities to fly, and

In taking time to formulate a considered and well-planned response to violations of the agreements committed by Iraq, the CAOC was able to 'make the punishment fit the crime'. In this sequence, taken from an F-15E's AAQ-14 target pod as the jet strikes its RO target, a suspected Scud missile propellant factory explodes in spectacular fashion (*USAF via author*)

they would typically go aloft at least four times a week in two to three combat sorties and one or two CTs.

The F-15E community was doubly fortunate. It was not only able to hone its air-to-air skills during CT sorties, but it could also maintain air-to-ground proficiency on OSW missions by practising simulated attacks when there were no ROs.

Container sorties were usually executed by a four-ship flight of F-15Es tasked to patrol a geographically prescribed 'container'. If they spotted a no-fly zone violation they reported it to await further instructions from the CAOC, which decided whether to execute any one or more of the ROs. Pilots and WSOs usually took off with imagery of three or four RO target areas, although it was unusual for more than a single RO to be executed on any given sortie.

Alert sorties were, by definition, less proactive and more reactive. Aircrew remained dressed in full flight gear (flight suit, g-suit, parachute harness and survival vest) for the duration of the 12-hour shift. This was notoriously uncomfortable, but essential if they were to be strapped in and ready to taxi within two to three minutes of receiving the call

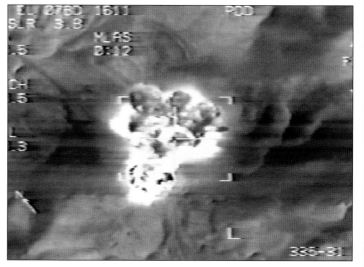

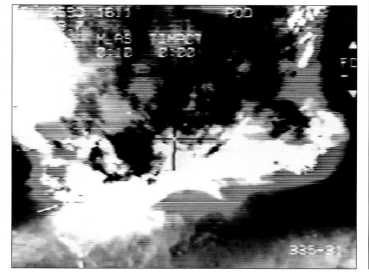

Cluster bomb units (CBUs) were not often carried because of their somewhat indiscriminate nature. CBUs could, however, be effective against soft military targets, and were carried when deemed necessary. This rare photograph shows a CBU-laden 492nd FS F-15E from RAF Lakenheath on patrol over Iraq in the late 1990s (*Gary Klett via author*)

from the CAOC. Such calls usually came when either an aircraft or ground contact required further investigation. Typical loadouts in support of OSW included GBU-12s, GBU-10s, AGM-130s, AIM-120s and AIM-9s. The use of cluster bombs was rare because of the weapon's indiscriminate nature.

FDL AND AIR-TO-GROUND OPs

The evaluation of F-15E sorties in OSW saw the jet become an early recipient of Fighter Data Link (FDL). Indeed, the Strike Eagle force was equipped with the system *before* the F-15C (which was originally the top priority to receive it), the F-15E making its combat debut with FDL during the aircraft's impromptu participation in Operation *Enduring Freedom* (OEF) in Afghanistan in late 2001.

The Iraqis tended not to draw attention to themselves, and to limit their activities to times which offered the greatest chance of success. The threat was therefore mobile, and would rapidly re-position to avoid retaliatory attacks once detected. Such tactics represented something of a headache for the Strike Eagle until FDL arrived. The latter allowed the expeditious transfer of target coordinates and information between RC-135 *Rivet Joint*, E-8 J-STARS, F-15C, F-16, F-15E and E-3 AWACS as soon as a target was detected.

While most of the RO target sets were fixed in nature, such as ammunition bunkers and command and control facilities, Strike Eagles were tasked to attack mobile targets like towed 100 mm KS-19 AAA guns before they could move away. FDL therefore facilitated time-critical targeting (TCT) missions, permitting the F-15E to instantly locate targets and to 'hook' radar and IR weapons guidance systems directly onto the FDL-generated target. The Strike Eagle also benefited from the same air-to-air features which FDL would bring to the F-15C, further enhancing its excellent air-to-air capabilities.

21

THE 'DIRTY' DEID

In late 2002 US President George W Bush made clear his intentions to implement a regime change in Iraq. It therefore became obvious even to the most cautious observer that war with Saddam Hussein was now imminent. The 4th FW, stationed at Seymour Johnson AFB, in North Carolina, and the world's largest F-15E Strike Eagle operator, became increasingly aware that it was likely to be deployed as part of the military build-up in the Gulf region.

While it is likely that the wing's senior leadership were informed of a possible tasking as early as December 2002, official notification did not arrive until January 2003. Capt Randall Haskin remembers;

'I'm pretty sure the actual initial tasking came around Christmas. We were officially told it was going to happen on 27 December. The "prepare to deploy" order is just as good as the actual deployment order, so when it came down in January, preparations were complete by that point.'

With the December communiqué received, the OG (Operations Group) designated the 336th FS as the first squadron to deploy, and set about the necessary administrative and organisational tasks. The 'Rocketeers' stood-down so that their aircraft could be configured for war, and to allow squadron personnel to take care of last-minute formalities. The 4th FW then optimised the time left to prepare the remaining squadron – the 335th FS, nicknamed the 'Chiefs' – for the eventuality that it too would be called upon. The 'Rocketeers' had been deliberately chosen by the wing to be the first unit to deploy principally because it had been denied the opportunity – at the very last minute – to go to Afghanistan to participate in OEF the year before.

The 'Rocketeers'' deployment orders were cryptically referred to as *Coronet East 074*, with the unit's final destination being Al Udeid

With more than 90 F-15Es occupying the same ramp space, Seymour Johnson AFB in North Carolina really is the home of the Strike Eagle (*author/FJ Photography.com*)

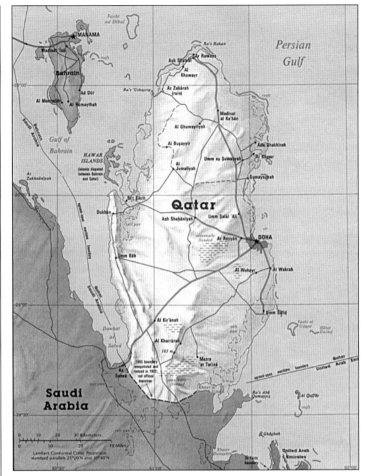

Although not marked on this CIA-issued map of Qatar, Al Udeid AB is centrally-located in the east of the country. Note Qatar's close proximity to both Saudi Arabia and the small island nation of Bahrain (*Central Intelligence Agency*)

AB, Qatar. While the operation's termination point was classified, the wing's TDY (Temporary Duty) orders very clearly stated that Al Udeid, Qatar, was its place of duty.

Al Udeid (pronounced 'Al-u-deed') had been custom-built in the 1990s by French contractors as a base for Qatari Air Force Mirage 2000 fighters. It also doubled as an attractive base for USAF KC-135 and KC-10 air refuelling tankers, and it is probable, given its scope and size, that the base was built by the Qataris with the United States firmly in mind. This certainly tied in with the suggestion that the Qatari government was keen to have Americans based on its soil to provide an element of security from hostile Arab nations.

Al Udeid's 15,000-ft runway was the longest in the Gulf region, and the base was home to the 379th Airborne Expeditionary Wing (AEW), the parent unit for all squadrons deployed to the base. The wing had seen a number of significant changes leading up to the war, moving from being a tanker unit to a mixed one of fighter aircraft, including RAF Tornado GR 4s and Australian F/A-18As. In fact, as the preparations progressed, four US Navy F-14As from USS *Kitty Hawk* (CV 63)-based VF-154 were also assigned to the AEW for a short time.

Al Udeid soon became known as 'the Deid', and later, as the sand penetrated everything, it became known as the 'dirty Deid'. Yet despite being of new design and construction, it was not well-suited to fighter operations, as the 4th FW's advance reconnaissance party soon discovered. Arriving in late December 2002 to evaluate the base for Strike Eagle operations, it found that the munitions dump was too small and that the refuelling points clustered around the tanker operations areas were not going to be of much use to hoards of fighters flying high sortie rates. On the other hand, as Capt Haskin noted;

'It's important to note that certain aspects of the base were superb. The airport facilities, such as runways, taxiways, ramps and airfield lighting were simply outstanding. The QRA (Quick Reaction Alert) stands were technologically amazing, with their low-observable faceted design and their ability to counter pressure and make them "clean" against chemical and biological attack. It was the support aspects which were severely lacking. The tents we were living and working in were quite austere. Once the 4th AEW rolled into town, we effected a significant number of

With war looming, 336th FS crews flew extensively to reach the optimum state of preparedness. When the official deployment order came in early January, the squadron was stood down. Seen flying an ACM sortie, and equipped with AIM-9M and AIM-120 drill rounds, this particular F-15E was later adorned with *Captain America* nose art once in the Gulf (*Randall Haskin via author*)

improvements to "Ops Town" especially. It was a strange dichotomy – a world-class airport facility with people living and working in tents next to the pavement!'

As the lead wing in the 379th, the 4th was also assigned to run the weapons and tactics shop as part of the operations support squadron (OSS). Lt Col Doug Reynolds of the 335th FS was the 4th FW's weapons and tactics officer, and was therefore tasked with managing the alterations necessary to make Al Udeid a better base for fighter operations. He was also made responsible for providing complete weapons and tactics support to all AEW tenant units.

Reynolds increased aviation fuel capacity from two to five million US gallons and improved the distribution facilities to allow hot refuelling at a number of points across the expansive ramp. He and his team also fashioned a new open-air weapons dump that separated the seven resident squadrons. Its ordnance was 'chronologically' stacked to allow easy weapons removal in accordance with the intended ATO so that those likely to be needed in the war's opening days were sited at the front. The existing secure weapons dump was not made available to the Coalition, so the 3.1 million pounds of weapons for the wing remained in the open.

CORONET EAST 074 DEPARTURE

Twenty-six 336th FS aircraft (two of which were air spares) were readied in the second week of January. Between the 11th and the 17th, all 24 assigned aircraft arrived at Qatar, via Moron AB, Spain, where they enjoyed a brief stop-over for crew rest. The capability to fly direct to Qatar certainly existed, however. Although 336th TFS crews had flown the 14-hour direct flight from Seymour Johnson to Dhahran, in Saudi Arabia, for the 1991 Gulf War, this deployment differed because the wing's entire support contingent was to co-locate alongside the aircraft

The 'Rocketeers' relied on a KC-10A tanker from Air Mobility Command's 6th Air Refueling Squadron/60th Air Mobility Wing to support their transatlantic crossing from Seymour Johnson to Moron AB, in Spain. The flight lasted some nine hours, and saw each F-15E complete several in-flight refuellings (*Randall Haskin via author*)

at the same time. Staggering the journey and implementing a building block approach made it easier to do this, although there were the expected hiccoughs.

Perhaps the most notorious was the Boeing 747 which had been chartered to carry 200+ support troops but which developed an engine oil leak in the early stages of its flight. The aircraft diverted to a northern European city, where its passengers disembarked and walked straight into a waiting media scrum. It would be another two days before they could fly out to join the rest of the 'Rocketeers'.

The crews, who included a small number of 335th FS pilots and WSOs assigned temporarily to the 336th to help bolster numbers, were given smallpox inoculations and then inducted into the current state of operations in the region. This essentially involved a briefing from CAOC planners in Saudi Arabia ('PSAB'), where the forthcoming battle was being planned under the auspices of OSW.

The latter had long been concerned with enforcing the southern no-fly zone, but had now metamorphosed into an operation oriented towards gathering intelligence on enemy positions and strengths, and initiating strikes on key Iraqi 'C3I' (command, control, communication and intelligence) sites and integrated air defence system nodes. The main topic of the briefing was OSW familiarisation and rules of engagement (ROE), but battlefield preparation for the forthcoming war was also briefly discussed.

Initially, the Strike Eagles were unable to contribute to this preparatory stage as they sat grounded at Al Udeid until 27 January 2003, when the US and Qatari governments finally concluded their diplomatic negotiations leading to the necessary permissions to fly. This delay was of real concern to the wing, even if it was not unexpected, as combat flying is a perishable skill. Senior 'Rocketeers' had suspected prior to arriving in-theatre that the host nation's different culture and thought processes need to be worked though before 'normal' operations could be resumed.

By all accounts getting checked out in local area procedures was something of a humorous affair. A Qatari Mirage 2000 pilot conducted the briefing, which included such gems as, 'You listen to me talk, or you no fly in Qatar', 'I am good pilot, trust me', 'Mirage 2000 Dash-5 is excellent airplane', and 'We can zoom up to 40,000 ft'. One WSO commented;

'The funny part was seeing the dudes from the 22nd EFS (F-16CJ squadron) sitting in the front row behaving themselves while this guy was talking. Then the quote came, "De Meer-aage two-thousand Daash five is excellent airplane, much like your American F-16 in many ways . . . just better! Ha Ha." At the time we Strike Eagle guys snickered, but you could actually hear the F-16 guys roll their eyes.'

The 'Rocketeers' soon discovered that Qatar operated fairly relaxed airspace procedures, even going so far as to permit flight in areas marked

on the map as prohibited. Despite this, Qatar lacked good quality military operating areas, and the 'Rocketeers' were unable to drop practice bombs as a result. Occasionally, they could practice coordinating with US Special Forces training Qatari commandos, but such opportunities were generally few and far between.

There were also administrative restrictions. The most peculiar was the Qatari insistence that all fighters going into Iraq would have to file an international (ICAO) flight plan using a local area call-sign which was to be used until leaving Qatari airspace. Once over Iraq the fighter could assume its tactical call-sign and get on with its mission. On return, the aircrew would once again use the local area call-sign, re-entering Qatar under civilian control. It is likely that these procedures existed to allow the government of Qatar to claim some form of plausible denial should other Gulf states kick up a fuss.

Saudi Arabia, which had long prohibited fighters with air-to-ground ordnance from routing through its airspace, maintained its tough stance. It even refused permission for Coalition strike aircraft to divert to its airfields in case of emergency. To make matters worse, F-15Es were forbidden from using established tanker tracks in the HONUS military operating area (MOA) in the north of the country for OSW.

Concerned by the threat of MANPADS Man-Portable Air Defence Systems) in the immediate vicinity of Al Udeid, a number of tactical departure and arrival routes were formulated and randomly flown. For example, the 'Stinger One' departure saw the pilot maintain 150 ft and 350 knots at the end of the runway, before aggressively pulling the nose up to 60 degrees at 400 knots. This climb was held until approximately 10,000 ft. Other profiles included the 'Chief One' arrival and the 'Rocket' departure, where expedience and minimised vulnerability to infra-red missiles were also the key objectives.

NTISR

When diplomatic permissions were eventually negotiated, the F-15E crews began flying strike familiarisation missions so as to become familiar with the OSW task. It was later that non-traditional intelligence surveillance and reconnaissance (NTISR) started as the OSW sortie count grew and the start of OIF drew closer. NTISR involved using the aircraft's onboard sensors – LANTIRN and LITENING pods, radar, fighter data link and ZSW-1 data link pod – to scour Iraq for targets of interest.

Home for three months in early 2003 – the first wave of F-15Es is seen parked at Al Udeid AB, Qatar, soon after arriving in the Gulf. Each aircraft is armed with live AIM-120 AMRAAMs. The dust and sand permeated everything, resulting in the base soon being christened 'The Dirty Deid' (*Randall Haskin via author*)

Predator UAVs and other aerial assets did their best to provide the CAOC with reconnaissance imagery, but the sheer volume of targets on which intelligence had to be gathered prompted the CAOC to ask for the F-15Es' assistance (*USAF*)

NTISR sorties were flown under the 'strike familiarisation' (or 'strike fam') banner, which meant that aircrew flew with live ordnance and with ROs ready to be executed should the CAOC send them the signal to strike a target while airborne. They were principally designed to allow a aircrew to familiarise themselves with ROE, local area procedures and flying over hostile territory before the commencement of all-out war.

NTISR involved the reconnoitering of specific targets or areas of suspected activity principally via the AAQ-14 or AAQ-28 FLIR targeting pod, but also using the APG-70 radar and the 'Mk 1 eyeball'. Intelligence personnel took the resulting pod/radar video and analysed it for tell-tale signs of activity, passing relevant video clips up the chain of command to the CAOC for further analysis. At this time the CAOC was still using the OSW system of dividing Iraq into large swathes of land named after US states. West to east, they were California, Texas, Ohio and Maine.

Capt Joe Siberski, an Instructor WSO with the 'Rocketeers', was assigned to the CAOC during OSW. He recalled;

'NTISR as I knew it started when I was at the CAOC. One day this intel captain comes up to me with an idea that he had already pitched to some "higher-ups". Apparently they had bought it, and now he was trying to make it work. His idea – I don't know if it was an original thought or not – was that we would recce places on our "strike fams" with the pods. He said he couldn't get conventional assets over a fraction of the sites he wanted with the timeline he needed, but we "Strikes" (F-15Es) flew over them all the time. So he bounced some ideas off me. I gave him my opinion and *voila*, it's in the "frag" the next day. He was a real cool dude, and sharp as all hell. I don't think he ever slept. I don't know how he did it. Even though he was so overworked, he always managed to find time to help me out whenever I needed intel assistance.'

Instructor WSO Capt Joe Siberski was assigned to the CAOC in Saudi Arabia during the final weeks of OSW (*author/FJ Photography.com*)

When not flying, the 'Rocketeers' busied themselves preparing attack profiles against the 40-odd targets they would be tasked to strike on the first night of the war. They had initially been briefed on the first six or so before leaving Seymour Johnson, and there was plenty of time to fine-tune their planning in the desert. Among the targets slated for destruction were cable repeaters in Baghdad. They were used by the Iraqi regime to communicate over long distances and, interestingly, by the time the 335th FS 'Chiefs' deployed, the target set had grown to as many as 150. These so-called 'manhole cover' targets would have been among the most difficult to hit due to their small size.

In the weeks leading up to OIF, the 'Rocketeers' would simulate striking sets of coordinates selected arbitrarily whilst on their way home from OSW missions. Sometimes they also practiced on bona fide cable repeater sites on the road from Basra below the 32nd parallel.

SCAR

Within days of commencing flight operations from Qatar, the 336th FS was formally asked to begin practicing strike coordination attack and reconnaissance (SCAR) sorties. Officially at least, this represented a new tasking for the squadron, although Lt Col Reynolds' wing weapons and tactics team had looked at the issues involved before leaving North Carolina following a tip-off from Ninth Air Force HQ in late December 2002. This research was headed by Maj Mark Thompson.

The intention was to enable all platforms in the area to kill the enemy effectively and efficiently. The US Navy's F/A-18s and F-14s had flown this hunter/killer role for a number of years, and it was their work that acted as the starting point for the Strike Eagle's foray into this new role. SCAR proved to be one of the areas in which the jet excelled, with its twin engines, two-man crew, superb sensors, long range, large weapons load and the ability to link in digitally with other assets (including C3I) being among the most obvious factors in its favour.

The US Navy led the USAF in its implementation of a fully blown FAC(A) programme. F-14s and F/A-18s had flown many FAC(A) missions in OEF in Afghanistan in 2001-02, and would subsequently fly many more during OIF. Their expertise and knowledge acted as the springboard for the F-15E's foray into SCAR (*US Navy*)

Flying along at medium altitude, the F-15E was not only required to hand off the target to the strike aircraft, but also to perform a positive identification (PID) to ensure the target was hostile. The crew was also expected to make a collateral damage estimate (CDE) to quantify the likelihood of friendly or civilian casualties based on the known blast effect of weapons that might be employed. Not only did this place a huge responsibility on the pilot and WSO, it was also a role for which they had never trained. Teaching aircrew to do this in peacetime is a

time-consuming and drawn-out process. It is even more impressive that the 336th FS embraced the challenge ahead of them and quickly became skilled at it.

SCAR placed the burden of responsibility on F-15E crews for finding, identifying, evaluating for collateral damage and handing-off targets to other strike platforms as they entered the area. It was very similar to the forward air controller (airborne) (FAC(A)) role, although there were no friendly troops in physical contact with the enemy. The big difference was that SCAR platforms cannot clear other aircraft 'hot' to attack targets. Capt Haskin summarised the difference between SCAR and FAC;

'The phraseology we had to use was, "cleared to engage", because we were not qualified as FACs. Cleared to engage meant the attacking aircraft still had the burden of PID and CDE.'

Capts Rich Meziere (pilot) and Christian Burbach (instructor WSO) of the 335th FS had both flown over Afghanistan the year before in support of OEF. It was an experience they believed had prepared them

and their 'Chiefs' colleagues well for the challenge of mastering the SCAR role. Burbach said;

'When we got back from Afghanistan we carried on flying TCT (Time Critical Target) missions rather than any of that pre-planned *Red Flag* stuff, so we were well-prepared for SCAR when the war kicked off. We had not even heard of the term "SCAR" until November 2002, but we soon found out that the TCT stuff we had done in Afghanistan was very transferable to it.'

Meziere added;

'When we deployed to Afghanistan only 16 per cent of our squadron had any kind of CAS (Close Air Support) or TCT experience (dropping live weapons in a CAS environment or in response to a TCT tasking). By the time we left that figure had become 96 per cent.'

The 'Chiefs' were clearly well-prepared for the challenge. They held an advantage over the 'Rocketeers' that would ultimately lead to the selection of a small number of them for highly-classified special operations 'on call' support missions.

OSW INTEGRATION

The 'Rocketeers' had deployed knowing that they would probably not see action until the proverbial 'Night One', when they would be going in cold after a lay-off of several weeks at Al Udeid. Briefed that the war would not start until mid-March, wing leadership wanted to secure as much operational flying as possible before the conflict kicked off. Lt Col 'Cowboy' Hughes was therefore sent to CAOC to act not only as a liaison officer between the CAOC and F-15E, but also to secure some part of the OSW action for the Strike Eagle community.

Once integrated into the OSW mission structure and daily ATO, Hughes then concentrated on getting ROs for his crews. This was no mean feat, for ROs were considered secondary to all other flying

JDAM was the primary weapon of choice for the CAOC during the last weeks of OSW, being dependable, simple to use and leaving little scope for user error (*USAF*)

operations at the time such as Defensive Counter-Air (DCA) and intelligence collection, and the CAOC, justifiably, had no tolerance for bombs going astray. Their weapon of choice, therefore, was JDAM.

As the squadron engaged in SCAR practice, CAOC simultaneously tasked it with executing several OSW ROs. Unfortunately, a handful of bombs went awry and the CAOC – under a political spotlight of extreme intensity – wanted to know why. On one occasion a 'Flat Face' early warning (EW) radar on the Jordan/Iraq border was marked for destruction. Two F-15Es located the site, but the first did not drop due to the weather over the target. The other mistakenly struck a nearby re-supply building. On another, a 'Pluto' EW radar was targeted, but two flights of F-15Es failed to completely destroy it in two separate strikes – the second was a GBU-24 strike. A B-1B was tasked to hit it with a Joint Direct Attack Munition (JDAM) on the third night, which it did successfully.

While misses are inevitable even with the best planning, ROEs and circumstances beyond the control of Strike Eagle crews had exacerbated the situation. The GBU-24 LGB briefly fell out of favour with the CAOC after the second 'Pluto' miss according to Lt Col Reynolds. The weapon had proved complex to master in Afghanistan the year before, an in its first ever use, the thermobaric version had missed a cave entrance following a high-risk planning strategy that had given the bomb a 900 ft margin to clear a ridge protecting the cave. There had also been numerous misses with the GBU-24 dating back to Operation *Allied Force* in the Balkans.

The crux of the matter was that the F-15E had been 'sold' to the CAOC as a platform equal to any JDAM dropper, and that it could hit the same targets just as well. When they were missed, CAOC wanted to know why. In the end a JDAM mentality emerged. This meant that if the pod cued to an area without a target under the cursors, then the Strike Eagle did not drop. If the WSO had to move his cursors to get to what he thought was his target, then he would not drop. 'For the controlled, critical climate of OSW, I think this was good ROE', commented one F-15E WSO.

Even though this GPS mentality made many WSOs feel they could not do their jobs by interpreting what they saw in the pods, they listened to their DO (Director of Operations) and CC (Squadron Commander) saying, 'Shut-up and colour. Don't get buck-fever because there will be plenty of bomb dropping to do later when the big one kicks off'.

Strike Eagles continued to be called upon for key elements of the preparation for war. Indeed, there were far more successes than failures, and the 'Rocketeers' struck radio relay stations, C3I posts, Integrated Air Defence System (IADS) nodes and leadership targets with alacrity. On one night alone, four F-15Es dropped GBU-24s (which had been given another chance) into the Republican Guard/Baath Party HQ in Basrah. Another four-ship

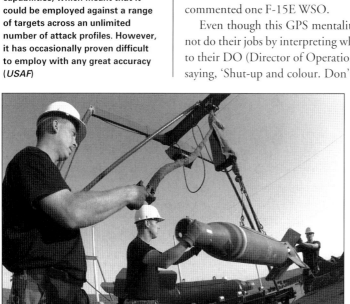

The GBU-24 advanced low-level Paveway III LGB offered tremendous capabilities, which meant that it could be employed against a range of targets across an unlimited number of attack profiles. However, it has occasionally proven difficult to employ with any great accuracy (*USAF*)

Strike Eagle flight flattened an air defence sector HQ in the same vicinity with six GBU-10s. Finally, the only GBU-28 drop of the war (which had actually been an OSW RO, and was only later included in OIF statistics) was a huge success that grabbed everybody's attention. The Strike Eagle was the only jet able to employ the weapon so far west, and it gave CAOC good cause to praise the 336th FS.

OPLAN 1003 VICTOR

On 7 February, 4th FW CO Brig Gen Eric J Rosborg arrived to take command of the 379th AEW at Al Udeid AB. The wing had grown rapidly and it now controlled the F-16CJs of the 22nd FS/52nd FW, RAAF F/A-18Cs, KC-135s, KC-10s and RAF Tornado GR 4s, in addition to the F-15Es. A group of F-117s arrived the next day.

Rosborg made his presence felt immediately. He ordered the construction of an officers' club in which rowdy fighter aircrew could let off steam without offending the base's other inhabitants. Vulgar songs and bullish drinking games have always been a part of the fighter pilot culture, and are accepted as part and parcel of the job. Rosborg wisely felt it would be good for morale to provide a suitable venue for these traditions to be maintained. In fact, near the end of OIF he went as far as to order the construction of a 15-ft concrete wall around the club to further contain the fun and games. Rumour has it that he jokingly observed, 'If I can't lock the criminals up, I'll at least contain them!'

Rosborg was viewed by many as a good leader who allowed his troops to conduct their mission. He led from the front from the moment he arrived, flying many combat missions over Iraq during the war often as a wingman, and he never pulled rank to override the flight lead's decisions. The O club was also a place to relax, and it is said that 'Chiefs' CO Lt Col 'Spanky' Dennis could often be found humming along to his favourite song, 'It's Raining Men', as it played on the jukebox in the background!

On the same day that Brig Gen Rosborg arrived, Operational Plan (OPLAN) 1003V was briefed to the 'Rocketeers'' resident pilots and WSOs. OPLAN 1003V ('ten-oh-three-victor') defined how the coalition would initiate full-scale ground and air-operations to unseat the Iraqi dictatorship. It was derived from OPLAN 1003-98, which had last been modified in 1998, as an 'off the shelf' defence plan should Iraqi forces once again attempt to occupy Kuwait. Two days later, on 9 February, the squadron received its brief-

Tanking during another OSW NTISR mission, this jet is noteworthy because it is actually a 335th FS machine. In addition to aircrew, the 336th FS also borrowed several airframes from its sister squadron for the initial deployment. These were handed back when the 'Chiefs' arrived in-theatre in late February 2003 (*Randall Haskin via author*)

Al Udeid AB was home to no less than six fighter squadrons from three nations. These 'bombless' RAF Tornado GR 4s of No 12 Sqn are seen at the 'last chance ramp', ready to taxi out onto the runway, in the final weeks of OSW (*Randall Haskin via author*)

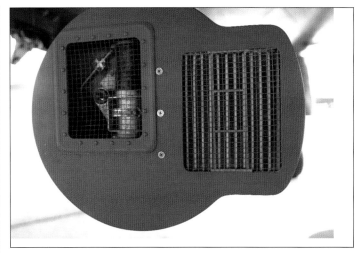

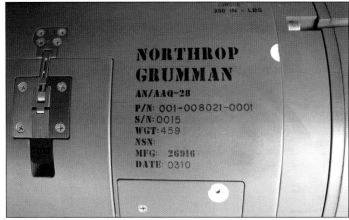

A Northrop Grumman AN/AAQ-28 Litening II pod loaded on a 'Chiefs'' jet. The pod is slightly fatter than the Lockheed Martin AAQ-14, and it also has a different optical assembly at the front (*author/FJ Photography.com*)

ing from the wing ground liaison officer, who explained how the ground war would unfold when the order to war finally came.

Towards the end of February, the 336th FS received additional aircrew so that the unit now comprised over 150 WSOs and pilots, many of whom were drafted in from the two Fighter Training Unit squadrons at Seymour Johnson (333rd FS and 334th FS) and the 391st FS at Mountain Home. The increased intake had been expected, and was necessary to satisfy the 2.0 crew ratio ordered by the CAOC. It also meant there were four aircrew for every Strike Eagle in-theatre.

As crews continued to fly SFAM (Strike Familiarity) sorties and conduct NTISR, the 335th FS 'Chiefs' at Seymour Johnson also deployed to Al Udeid, bringing the total number F-15Es at the Qatari base to 55.

The need for laser eye protection was one consideration as the proposed start date of the war – 19 March – drew nearer. It was well documented in classified and open source reports that the threat of instantaneous or delayed blindness to aviators illuminated by lasers was real. Intelligence briefed the 'Rocketeers' and 'Chiefs' that Iraqi forces were using up-rated commercial lasers, fixed to AK-47 assault rifles, to aim at aircraft passing overhead. At least one F-16 pilot had suffered damaged vision following a sortie over Iraq in the years before and some F-15E aircrew elected to wear eye protection glasses (called Clear Laser Eye Protection for Infra Red and Ruby), which both squadrons had hurriedly sourced from a UK manufacturer. As the war

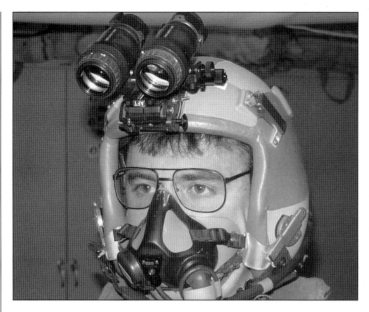

CLEPIR glasses were carried by most crewmembers, although they were rarely worn (*Randall Haskin via author*)

progressed, few aircrew actually elected to wear their glasses for flight, although many carried them just in case.

NEW PODS

Also new to both squadrons was a limited supply of the Northrop Grumman AN/AAQ-28 targeting pod, which was an enhanced version of the original Lockheed Martin AAQ-14. The AAQ-28 – better known as Litening II (LII) Advanced Target Pod – featured a laser spot tracker and optical sensor, in addition to an improved derivative of its predecessor's FLIR sensor. These additional systems allowed better daytime operation and extended range target acquisition capabilities, as well as facilitating coordination with other ground and airborne laser designators. However, the LII's IR sensor was inferior to that fitted in the AAQ-14 in some respects, as was later to become clear.

The new pod also required less maintenance support because it had no slip ring to allow the electronics and optical assemblies in the nose to move freely in any direction. The slip ring had proven to be a maintenance nightmare, and it was replaced in the LII by a wiring loom that could be coiled to allow the optics to rotate freely, but which had to 'de-roll' once it had coiled/rotated more than 425 degrees. Despite the pod's increased supportability, there was a critical caveat that lessened its overall impact on the war. The problem with the AAQ-28 was that the 4th FW was not permitted to maintain them, as Instructor WSO Capt Burbach explained;

'The technical representative from Northrop Grumman was the only guy allowed to troubleshoot them, and he couldn't get into the country for some reason. So we had 18 or 19 of these pods, but between the two squadrons we had only six to nine that actually worked.'

The de-roll process, which could occur without warning to the crew, would spin the seeker head back to its neutral setting to uncoil the wire bundle. In the weeks to come, at least one aircrew would be actively lasing a target with the bomb in flight when the pod decided to de-roll. Capt Siberski explained;

'The de-roll bit me a couple of times. It wasn't like I didn't know about it or that I wasn't checked out on the pod properly. The problem occurred when we were in dynamic targeting environments without a pre-planned attack and we executed a dive-glide, or dive-toss attack. In a dive-glide/dive-toss attack the pilot rolls inverted and pulls, which potentially does two things. Firstly, (geometry dependant) the pilot may visually check the designation in the HUD. Secondly, diving at the target gives the WSO some extra time to acquire (or identify) the target in the pod so that we can deliver ordnance and not "go through dry" on the first pass.

'Getting a bomb off on each pass can be critical when gas is tight and the natives are getting restless. With a Litening pod, when you roll and pull, it wraps up the pod and you can usually get down the chute, deliver the bomb and start the designator leg. But it will usually hit the limit (and de-roll) some time before impact as you pass the target, causing a miss. We can bunt instead of rolling, but we don't normally like to bunt. Negative G is bad, and stuff starts flying around the cockpit. It's more natural and more effective to roll. The roll limit can also bite you in a CAS environment, where the "wheel" tactic is used.

'Wheeling around the target area is more of a visual tactic, but I usually put the pod on the target, which would wrap up. To counter this, you can execute a "modified racetrack" or "bowtie" orbit. In conclusion, I thought the LII's roll limit sucked eggs, but we learned to cope with it by just not rolling.'

One small bonus that Litening II brought to the WSO in particular was the manner in which the picture was orientated on the MPD. The image rotated within the display as the aircraft's position relative to the target changed. Siberski commented;

'It had something to do with the way the image is processed, coupled with the fact that the new pods had an internal INU (Inertial Navigation Unit) for tracking/coordinate reference. I didn't even notice it after a while, but it gave a little SA (Situational Awareness) on how we were moving about the target when I was stuck heads-down at night.'

FINAL ROs

The CAOC continued to task ROs in the final weeks of OSW. One particular objective was to take down Iraq's early warning network along the border with Jordan. This was an important objective, as OPLAN 1003V required US F-16s and Special Forces helicopters to operate out of Jordan once hostilities began in earnest. The earlier ROs to target the 'Pluto' and 'Flat Face' radars had formed part of this objective, and, accordingly, several radar sites and radio relay antennae were struck near

This 'Chiefs' F-15E boasts an AN/AAQ-28 pod beneath its port engine intake. Seen on a post-war training mission from Seymour Johnson, it also carries an AIM-120 drill round

Right above
E-3 AWACS platforms were airborne literally 24 hours a day during OSW, and they kept a watchful eye on IrAF activity at all times. With a few notable exceptions, things were generally quiet (*USAF*)

the H-3 airfield and across the length of the border. These missions met heavy AAA opposition, and there were known SA-13 and Roland SAM sites whose weapon engagement envelopes protected the Strike Eagle's assigned targets.

On one occasion, three Strike Eagles flew west of H-3 to strike S-60 AAA and mobile Roland SAM batteries. While the S-60s were successfully dispatched, the Roland escaped unharmed after AWACS passed the lead aircraft new coordinates in flight. In the ensuing engagement, the new coordinates matched what looked like a Roland launcher, but the pod video later showed it to be a small missile support building of some kind. Post-strike satellite imagery showed the Roland sitting safely at the original position briefed by the 'Rocketeers' intelligence officer.

The IrAF continued to fly its own training sorties within the sanctity of the airspace north of the 32nd Parallel and south of the 35th in the final weeks of OSW. MiG-25s, MiG-23s and Mirage F1EQs would often venture to the edge of the southern no-fly zone before crossing it briefly or heading back home well short of the line. On more than one occasion, F-15Es flying DCA patrols were alerted to the presence of airborne threats, which they tracked on

Flying high above the southern Iraqi no-fly zone, this 58th FS F-15C from Eglin AFB, Florida, moves slowly away from the tanker following an in-flight refuelling. It is armed with six AIM-120 AMRAAMs and two AIM-9M Sidewinder missiles (*USAF*)

radar and Fighter Data Link, certain that Iraq was about to launch its own pre-emptive attack against the Coalition.

Once, in early March, upwards of ten Iraqi fighters simultaneously became airborne as two U-2s flew overhead Baghdad conducting reconnaissance in accordance with a UN agreement with Saddam Hussein. This agreement required all other Coalition fighters to be out of the no-fly zones, so when a startled AWACS controller detected five groups of fighters getting airborne there was real concern for the U-2s' safety. They beat a hasty retreat and AWACS cleared F-15Es and F-15Cs flying DCA south of the Iraqi border to engage should the IrAF jets enter the no-fly zone. In the event, it became apparent that the Iraqis were simply conducting their last few flights before the outbreak of full-scale war. Indeed, those Strike Eagle aircrew who were airborne and ready to protect the U-2s have characterised these flights as the Iraqi pilots' 'fini' flights.

The complete lack of Iraqi activity following the execution of OPLAN 1003V has prompted many to wonder if some kind of 'arrangement' had not previously been secretly negotiated by US or British intelligence agencies with senior IrAF officers. Others, though, take the view that self-preservation simply took over once the war started.

WATCHFUL EAGLES

F-15C Eagles of the 71st and 94th FSs/1st FW, from Langley AFB, Virginia, and the 58th FS/33rd FW, at Eglin AFB, Florida, deployed to the region in support of OIF in February and March 2003. The 13 aircraft and 22 pilots of the 58th FS 'Gorillas' moved on 6 March 2003 to King Faisal Air Base, in Saudi Arabia, while the 71st FS deployed an identical number of personnel and aircraft to Incirlik AB, in Turkey.

The Eagles flew the same sort of ONW and OSW DCA sorties as was described in chapter two, but there was no trade for them in the final weeks of OSW/ONW, or for the entire duration of OIF. In fact, the 94th flew the last ever ONW sortie on 17 March, two days before the war began. Since the operation's inception, and the unit's subsequent inability to fly combat missions over Iraq from Turkey, the 94th worked to redeploy its forces or to bring them home. There was even some talk of redeployment to support the war effort from one of the many Saudi bases, but eventually the squadron returned home.

The last F-15C unit to deploy to Saudi Arabia was the Okinawa-based 67th FS/18th FW, led by Lt Col Matt Molloy. It flew five Eagles into 'PSAB' from Kadena AB, Okinawa, in December 2002 as part of the routine Air Force Expeditionary Forces schedule. Initially assigned to OSW to enforce the no-fly zone in southern Iraq, the squadron was fully engaged in OIF with the 363rd AEW from mid-March.

A 94th FS F-15C refuels from a USAF tanker over the Mediterranean during the immediate build up to OIF. This unit was committed to ONW at the time, and following the cessation of this operation in mid March it soon returned home to Langley AFB (*USAF*)

A total of five F-15Cs from the Kadena-based 18th FW had deployed to Prince Sultan AB, in Saudi Arabia, to fly with the 363rd AEW as part of PACAF's OSW commitment in December 2002. Remaining in-theatre throughout OIF, the fighters, drawn from the 67th FS, were not permitted to participate in offensive missions into Iraq during the war (*USAF*)

Complete air supremacy over Iraq was declared within days of the war commencing, following which the 67th FS 'Fighting Cocks' returned home after logging more than 4000 combat hours and 700 combat missions. The squadron had been the sole Pacific Air Forces F-15 unit to participate in OIF.

The two F-15C squadrons (the 71st and the 58th) working the OSW commitment with the 358th AEW out of Sheikh Isa, in Bahrain, also returned home early, well aware that their presence was no longer needed. The 58th departed for Eglin AFB on 25 April, having flown 2046.5 combat hours and achieved an 83 per cent mission capable rate. By the time the 71st got back to Langley AFB it had been deployed for a little over two months. With the departure of the F-15Cs, the DCA role was quickly assumed by other in-theatre platforms, including the F-15E.

The Kingdom of Saudi Arabia permitted USAF F-15s to operate from its air bases purely because they had been tasked to fly in a defensive role. These 58th FS F-15Cs are seen taxiing out to the runway at King Faisal AB prior to taking off on another OSW DCA patrol (*USAF*)

Back home. The lack of resistance from the IrAF freed these 1st FW C-model F-15s to head back to Langley AFB earlier than originally anticipated. This photograph was taken upon the jets' arrival in Virginia (*USAF*)

NON-TRADITIONAL WARFARE

Col Daryl Roberson was the individual responsible for the Strike Eagle wing's deployment. A veteran F-15E pilot who flew in the 1991 Gulf War, he was 4th FW Operations Group (OG) CO and 379th AEW OG deputy CO. Having overseen both units' deployment, he arrived in-theatre in March 2003 and assumed responsibility for the OG's night shift. The 379th OG CO from Cannon AFB, Col Charles Dodd, ran the day shift. One Strike Eagle pilot commented;

'It's interesting to note that Dodd, being an F-16 guy, wasn't all that impressed with the F-15E when he first got there, and he repeatedly made fun of the two-seat jet. After the war was over, and he'd seen all the ass we'd kicked, he had changed his tune!'

The OG existed to help the squadrons assigned to the group with resources and coordination with the CAOC. Roberson explained;

'We were there to help with the integration of the squadrons into the system. They were very resourceful and had brought all of their leadership with them, so it was fairly simple for the most part.'

Moreover, Roberson was responsible for making decisions relating to sortie generation, operational employment of the aircraft, weapons selection and maintaining the resources necessary to be successful. His team was also responsible for passing on squadron feedback to CAOC. Roberson added;

'The CAOC took the information that we provided, then moulded it to fit the ATO according to the requirements from the commander. We then took the "frag" from the CAOC and made sure that we were able to execute it. If we couldn't, then we'd review it and massage it so that we could execute the mission. The CAOC had the big picture. The OG allocated the resources to accomplish and execute the mission.'

Planning for the CAOC and the OG was complicated by Turkey, which rescinded permission for the US to operate offensively out of Incirlik. While the 4th FW had never been destined to operate from this base, it soon found itself being assigned to areas of operation in northern Iraq which might have been the responsibility of other coalition aircraft based in Turkey – it has been suggested that the 48th

A Strike Eagle is prepared for battle in the days leading up to OIF. The F-15E would go on to attain the second-highest mission-capable rate of all the USAF's strike and fighter assets in-theatre once the conflict started (*USAF*)

FW at RAF Lakenheath may have been set to send some of its F-15Es to Turkey prior to the cessation of ONW and the implementation of Turkish airspace restrictions. The OG was also involved in helping the CAOC to continually modify OPLAN 1003V. Following a brief indoctrination by the CAOC, Fighter Weapons School graduates in each squadron, the OG and each squadrons' mission planning cells (MPCs) dry-ran the flow of the first few nights' taskings to ensure that the rolling, escalating, plan could be properly executed.

OIF BEGINS

As it came earlier than originally intended, there remains confusion about when OSW ceased and OIF started. The issue is complicated by OSW procedures and ROEs being phased out and gradually replaced by OIF procedures and ROEs over the course of a 24-hour period. From an aircrew perspective, the new ROE and special instructions (SPINS) were drastically simplified in comparison with those observed during OSW.

For example, OSW prohibited crews from striking a target unless it was within 50 ft of the coordinates supplied by the CAOC. OIF ROE allowed any target within an assigned kill box to be struck,

The GBU-28 'bunker buster' was the first bomb dropped during OIF, the weapon being used successfully against a key node in the Iraqi IADS just hours before the F-117s struck presidential palaces (*USAF and Steve Davies/FJ Photography.com*)

provided that PID and CDE were met, and there were no friendly ground units reported in the area. In fact, the OIF ROE and SPINS had been handed down to the crews in mid-February, but they had been actively discouraged from reading them in the hope that they would not accidentally apply OIF ROE to an OSW mission.

It was immediately after a successful GBU-28 strike on the Intercept Operations Centre at H-3 by four F-15Es on 19 March that two F-117s, call-sign 'Ram 01' and 'Ram 02', headed north at 0500Z at short notice to strike a target believed to house Saddam Hussein. As the F-15Es returned from what has now been classed as the first OIF sortie, their radios came alive and blocks of airspace were cleared by AWACS to allow passage for incoming Tomahawk land attack cruise missiles. As still more F-15E crews made their way north into Iraq in order to execute ROs and man DCA stations, they received word that their refuelling assets had been re-tasked – to support the two F-117s heading for Baghdad, it later transpired. Capt Haskin commented;

'When I called AWACS to hook up with my tanker, I wasn't happy to hear them tell me that my tanker was no longer available for my flight, and that "all gas is currently in support of 'Ram 01' package". I just had no clue at the time who this 'Ram 01' was!'

Groundcrews prepare two of the eight AGM-130 missiles employed by F-15Es on the first night of OIF to strike transportation facilities used exclusively by Saddam Hussein and his sons (*USAF*)

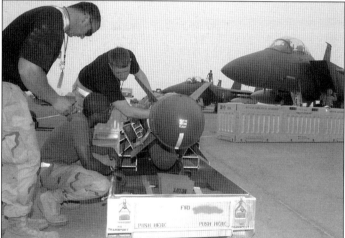

The CAOC had originally asked for these opportunistic targets to be struck by the F-15E using the AGM-130, but the lengthy and involved planning necessary for such a strike precluded its use. The mission therefore fell to the two F-117s and their EGBU-27 bombs. Burbach explained, 'They wanted the AGM-130 because of the video that we'd have brought back showing the missiles hitting the target. They wanted that for CNN'.

AGM STRIKES

The first full day of the war saw experienced Strike Eagle crews from both squadrons tasked with launching AGM-130 strikes against key leadership targets. Four Strike Eagles from each squadron carried a single weapon on one shoulder pylon, a ZSW-1 IDLP on the centre, a 600-gallon fuel tank on the other shoulder pylon, two GBU-12s on the left CFT, two AIM-120s on the right CFT and three AIM-9s on the shoulder missile pylons. A fourth AIM-9 could not be carried because of fin clearance issues, so an AIM-120 was loaded instead.

Primed and loaded, an AGM-130 sits ready to go – the bomb has been suitably adorned with messages to the Iraqi dictator from those sent to dethrone him. The (yellow) stripe around the body of the bomb denotes that it contains a live warhead, while the (brown) stripe immediately below it indicates the fitment of a live rocket motor (*Randall Haskin via author*)

The 'Chiefs' were tasked with striking Republican Guard barracks near Baghdad International Airport, while the 'Rocketeers' were to go after Saddam Hussein's yacht club. Both targets formed part of the Iraqi dictator's personal transportation infrastructure, and were chosen to make it harder for him to flee the city in the coming hours.

The AGM-130 used a modified GBU-15 bomb as the basis for an extended range precision guided munition (PGM). A rocket motor was mounted on the underside to provide the bomb with a glide-boost-glide operating profile. The motor was not intended to accelerate the bomb, but simply to maintain a desired minimum velocity so that once it had used up its fuel the powerplant would be jettisoned automatically. AGM-130-9/-10/-11/-12 variants also featured a GPS mid-course guidance system which allowed the bomb to navigate towards the target area. In the latter two versions an additional antenna was installed in the bomb to help increase IDLP reception coverage – a feature known as switchable data link.

Electro-optical (EO) and infra-red versions of the AGM-130 used the WGU-40/B television guidance section and WGU-42/B improved modular infra-red sensor seeker heads respectively. Both seekers had a 4.2-degree vertical by 5.6-degree horizontal field of view. Gimbal limits were plus 30 degrees to minus 54 degrees pitch and plus or minus 30 degrees yaw.

The weapon functioned like the GBU-15, although the AGM-130 could be programmed with its own transit altitude to allow target entry as low as 200 ft or as high as 2000 ft. The central computer automatically calculated the dynamic launch zone based on the user selection, and a missile-mounted radar altimeter provided elevation data.

When the weapon was deployed in indirect mode, the aircrew could subsequently designate a target in the aircraft via the TGT FLIR or High-Resolution Map (HRM) radar mode. The target data would be transmitted to the AGM-130, which would compute the target location relative to its own. A small triangle would be superimposed over the AGM-130 video in the

cockpit to provide the WSO with steering cues to help him guide the weapon to the target. Narrow and wide FOVs were provided for enhanced target acquisition purposes. AGM-130 launches usually worked with two aircraft monitoring video imagery beamed back via the AXQ-14 or ZSW-1 DLP/IDLP. If the primary jet was unable to locate the target in a timely manner, the secondary one was used as a fallback. The primary crew would typically transmit; 'Goalkeeper, Goalkeeper' as a cue for the secondary crew to take control of the missile.

For these key attacks on the Iraqi dictator's private transportation infrastructure and hardware, pairs of aircraft each had a single target, and two weapons would be used against each.

As the eight Strike Eagles became airborne, it immediately became obvious that the mission was not going to go according to plan. Of the four 'Chiefs' aircraft, No 2 experienced an AGM-130 failure while still on the ground. No 1 launched its weapon successfully but the missile exploded moments after leaving the aircraft, possibly due to AAA fire. No 4 pickled the weapon but the release sequence failed and the battery squib did not fire the rocket motor, leaving the aircraft with a hung bomb.

The AGM-130's seeker head forms the subject for this striking self-portrait. The WGU-42B IMIRS (Improved Modular Infra-Red Set) was used on the air-to-ground missiles expended on the war's first night (*Gary Klett via author*)

Minutes before launching on the opening night of OIF, four 335th FS AGM-130-equipped jets sit ready to taxi. The mission would be hampered by technical problems associated with the Strike Eagles' ordnance (*USAF*)

Only No 3 had a successful guide to target. The 'Rocketeers' were even less successful, and all four of their weapons failed to destroy their targets.

The author understands that the 336th FS jets suffered a command data link problem, the AGMs beaming back their seeker images well enough but the command signals necessary for the WSOs to guide the weapons failing to work. There has been some speculation that nearby EA-6B Prowler jamming aircraft may have interfered with the command frequency, although some dismiss this out of hand due to the extensive coordination before the AGM-130 strikes. The AGM sorties had been meticulously planned but the AGM-130 had a reputation for being less reliable than desirable. These missions served to reinforce this perception.

'KICK-ASS'

Both squadrons had been tasked not only to provide the four AGM-130 aircraft but also a quartet of offensive counter air (OCA) jets. These air-to-air-optimised F-15Es were to push forward to quash any resistance from the IrAF. While none was found, at least one pair of Strike Eagles moved its orbit further south as withering AAA and unguided SAM launches lit up the sky. One pilot reportedly counted as many as 40 SAM launches in the war's first hour.

With the AGM and OCA F-15Es airborne, the remaining Strike Eagles entered Iraqi airspace to fly kill box interdiction (KI) and pre-planned precision strike sorties across the length and breadth of the country. Throughout the conflict, the Strike Eagle was the only Coalition aircraft to possess sufficient range and self-protection and target detection capabilities to allow it to roam freely in both northern and southern Iraq.

The whole 'shock and awe' OPLAN 1003V battle plan was scaled back as the F-117s went in early to destroy the bunkers believed to be housing Saddam Hussein and the Iraqi leadership. Coalition ground forces were forced to expedite their push northwards while they still held some element of surprise. Capt Randall Haskin remembers;

'My impression of this was that the attack plan was literally changed "on-the-fly" between the night of the Saddam strike by the F-117s and

Bombed up with nine GBU-12s and ready to roll out onto the runway at Al Udeid on the first full day of the war, this F-15E would probably have returned with most, if not all, of its weapons spent
(*Randall Haskin via author*)

what was supposed to be the actual "A-day" following the "shock and awe" night of the TLAM (Tomahawk Land Attack Missile) attacks.'

Capt Meziere recalled;

'What we all saw was a scaled back version of the original plan. When we were briefed on the original plan, everyone *was* shocked and awed. When we were then shown the follow-on plan, which outlined how quickly the Army and Marines were going to move when the first bombs fell, we thought that the whole situation on the ground and in the air was going to get pretty bad. As it turned out things went better than we had anticipated, but there were still some problems that we encountered later on as a result of the speed at which the Army moved.'

As the ground troops moved north at terrific pace, the F-15E community soon began to worry that Coalition units might be left exposed. One interviewee told the author, 'We jokingly started to call it "shock and awww-sh*t!" when it looked like the ground troops were spread too thin and got bogged down in An Nasiriyah and the like.'

With the Army moving so quickly ahead of the proposed start of 'shock and awe', very few F-15E 'lines' (the name given to the individual sorties handed down by the CAOC in the 'frag') were for fixed target, interdiction type missions. Most were for KI and on-call CAS support sorties. The correct term for these dual-role sorties was KI/CAS, which inevitably became known as 'kick-ass' – this would prove to be an apt term. KI involved patrolling 30-mile square grids defining a kill box, in which SCAR tactics were executed.

The F-15Es often flew at medium altitude searching for targets of opportunity. When targets were found the No 2 aircraft was sometimes the first to release ordnance. No 1 flew over the target and executed PID and CDE, then cleared No 2 – usually three miles behind – to drop. This had the additional advantage of reducing No 2's weapons load, allowing him to save fuel. Wingmen typically burn more than their leaders because they must manipulate the throttle more often to stay in formation. When No 1 was the first to drop, No 2 would often position so as to allow him to drop almost as soon as No 1 came off target. This was essentially the 'bow tie' attack pattern which, as Capt Siberski explained, was better suited to the AAQ-28.

It was during a KI/CAS mission on 3 April that three US servicemen were killed and five more injured when a 336th FS F-15E dropped a single GBU-12 weapon on a friendly position. The aircraft's pilot and WSO were cleared of any negligence by an enquiry which was initiated immediately afterwards. A broad sketch of events that night indicates that the incident happened immediately after the downing of an F/A-18C from USS *Kitty Hawk*-based VFA-195 by a US Patriot missile battery.

Apparently still unaware of the cause of that loss, US fighters in the area were keeping a watchful eye out for possible hostile MANPAD and SAM systems which might have been responsible. Seeing a suspicious target, the 'Rocketeers' crew called AWACS to ask if there were friendly forces in the area and got the response that there were none. The rest has been put down to the 'fog of war'.

The entire situation with Patriot missile batteries repeatedly threatening Coalition aircraft or actually firing on them, causing the deaths of two RAF Tornado aircrew and the F/A-18C pilot, is one that continues to

The Patriot PAC-3 missile battery caused Coalition airmen great concern, and scored two friendly-fire kills during OIF (*US Army*)

mystify. While it was clearly very important to have Patriot protection against Tactical Ballistic Missiles (TBMs) and other weapons of mass destruction-carrying systems, it was obvious to all concerned that the IrAF was not prepared to fight. Why then, with a non-existent air threat, were two Coalition aircraft attacked by Patriot batteries?

The threat posed by the Patriot had several undesirable effects on the way that the Strike Eagle and other fast jet communities operated. Firstly, it forced crews to actively squawk mode 2 IFF codes on their transponders, which could in turn be tracked by some SAM systems as a form of missile homing signal. Among those SAMs with this capability are two known to have been used by the Iraqi IADS. Secondly, it placed a great psychological strain on flyers operating within range of Patriot systems. Those aircrews who were locked-up by Patriots recall having the fear of God put into them. The usual response was to manoeuvre evasively, dump chaff and make a frantic call to AWACS.

'NO GAS KICK-ASS'

'No gas' KI/CAS missions were extremely popular variations of the 'kick-ass' mission, at least for the first couple of weeks of OIF. They were also extremely useful for the CAOC planners, who took advantage of the Strike Eagle's ability to get up to the kill box and conduct its mission without depending on a tanker for en route refuelling. These missions mostly saw the F-15E operating between Kut and Basra, from where the Army feared any counter-attack by the Iraqi Republican Guard was most likely to originate.

Such a counter attack was, by all accounts, a genuine concern for the Army and Marines, who soon found comfort from the protection afforded by the Strike Eagle. It certainly had the legs for the mission, but to optimise each aircraft's potential, the crews would 'double turn', having returned to Al Deid. This meant flying twice in one day, often returning from the first flight, grabbing a bite to eat, going to the ops desk to get the new jet's tail number and then going back to the original KI/CAS location. Capt Meziere recalls;

'We'd been tasked to fly up to the north of Basra without refuelling. Everything went according to plan until we got there. Then we got a call from AWACS that there was a suspected SSM (surface-to-surface missile) for us to find and kill. We knew we'd need gas to find this thing, especially as the weather was pretty bad. But I couldn't raise anyone on the radio to take gas from. I called everyone and got no reply. I'm sitting there thinking, "This is a pretty important mission and I can't even get gas". In the end we had to turn around and head home with all our bombs still attached. It was a pretty depressing experience.'

Clear in both of these photographs are the light grey 600-gallon war reserve materiel (WRM) drop tanks used by the F-15E during OIF. WRM tanks were cheap to make as they lacked some of the internal baffling of the 'genuine' article. They served as a cost-effective and expedient way of replacing tanks jettisoned in the heat of combat (*Randall Haskin via author*).

Meziere's experience was probably isolated, as many of the 'no gas kick-ass' missions were exciting and challenging to the aircrew.

For the first 11 days of the war, the 4th FW surged to maximum capacity and beyond, reaching an apogee of 96 sorties per day between the two squadrons. Col Roberson in the OG had been asked before the war to give an estimate for the duration of the wing's activities. He had responded as accurately as he could, but never in his wildest dreams did he expect that the groundcrew, aircrew and support infrastructure at the base could give so much for so long. The 'no gas kick-ass' mission was used most prolifically during this 11-day period.

With aerial tankers a precious commodity, F-15Es soon began flying into the Kuwait military airfield of Al Jaber to top up with fuel before undertaking more 'no gas kick-ass' missions even deeper into Iraq. Capt Haskin explained;

'The "Rocketeers" did quite a bit of hot-pitting at Al Jaber when the tanker assets were getting spread thin. When we did hot-pit through Jaber, those were the full-on missions up in central Iraq.'

The Republican Guard counter attack did eventually come south-east to the besieged city of Basra, but it was decimated by F-15Es and other Coalition fighter-bombers. This offensive was the only mass action attempted by the Iraqi Army during OIF, and it was said to have comprised over 100 vehicles and tanks.

Strike aircraft were urgently needed to blunt this assault, and Capt Siberski explained the technique employed by 4th FW crews to maximise their time over the approaching force;

'We could get up to Kut and Basra without refuelling, work for a little while, then fly home. Time is gas, gas is time, so we'd use the FDL to find who was coming back without bombs. FDL wouldn't just give us that, it would also give us their radio frequencies, so we'd call them up. In fact, if you had a good "co-ord card" (a coordination card issued by the CAOC to show all jets, call-signs and radio frequencies in use for a particular "frag") then you could actually work out who was in which aircraft. We'd figure out their auxiliary frequency and ask them, "Hey dudes, what have you got?" They'd reply, "Check out my mark points 3, 4 and 5. We didn't have enough bombs to get them all. The guy you want to talk to is this guy, don't go through this agency, talk to this one instead".

'Basically, we were getting really good gouge on how to get to the target area, and that allowed us to minimise our time holding while we tried to find the targets ourselves. We could then give the same hand-off to our other buddies, because the way it worked is that someone was usually checking into the area as you checked out of it.'

Strike Eagles often carried a mixed load of fusing combinations on the ubiquitous GBU-12 – instant fusing on one side, delayed on the other – to operate as flexibly as possible in a mixed-target environment. Capt Haskin explained;

'This was a decision made at the flight-lead level, which I think is notable. I was always under the impression as I trained for combat back in North Carolina that the ATO would specify things like fusing on bombs. After several days of flying in OIF with a nine-GBU-12 load out, and realising that the targets we were hitting were widely varied, someone also figured out that the ATO didn't seem to specify fusing – at least the version of it that we saw in the squadron didn't.

Armed with nine GBU-12s and on the boom of the tanker getting gas, an F-15E tops off its tanks before pressing north into Iraq. The jet had such good range that a tanker was usually only scheduled when flying up into central or northern Iraq (*USAF*)

'Some flight leads took the initiative to think of a plan to carry mixed fusing. They took the risk, and operationally it worked. Even better, nobody up the chain of command said anything about it, so more and more flight leads started doing this.'

On some occasions the ATO might task the crews with a primary mission that, it would transpire, could not be fulfilled or was superfluous to requirements. At that point the F-15E would default to SCAR .

Capt Siberski experienced at first-hand the advantages of carrying a mixed fused load on two 'no gas kick-ass' sorties that he flew with an A-10 FAC(A). He recalled;

'On this day we worked with an A-10 and an F-14D. We were in a kill box talking to the A-10 and he sent us to a place where there were some tanks and ammo storage bunkers to hit. We hit the tanks and then decided to put the rest of our bombs on the bunkers. They didn't look all that hardened, but sure enough our GBU-12s exploded on top of them. We ran out of gas and returned home (to Al Deid) thinking, "Damn, it's gotta' be those fuses that are causing the bombs to just explode like that."'

Siberski and his pilot double-turned and flew back to the kill box once again to talk to the new A-10 FAC(A).

'We had now cranked-up the fuses, turning up the delay so that the bombs would penetrate a little further before exploding. We checked in with the new FAC, but he was working a lot further west than before. He didn't have a pod (the A-10 force was issued with Litening II just prior to OIF), and he wanted to stay above the AAA, so he couldn't really find much for us, and there was nothing in the revetments that he'd pointing us towards. I eventually said to him, "Hey, when we were here earlier there were some targets further east. Can we go look over there?" He was a really good FAC(A), and he replied, "Sure", making a beano line to de-conflict us from some F/A-18s that he also had working for him. He sent them west and us east.

'Our No 2 guy had a Litening pod on his jet, and he found some more tanks for us to kill. We then took the cranked-up fuses and returned to the bunkers. Well, guess what? This time the bunkers erupted in huge fireballs. Woo hoo, secondaries! Almost at the same time as the bombs hit, the radio came alive and the FAC(A) said to us, "You guys can work over there if you want, but I really don't think there's anything to see". As soon as the explosions started, he was right back on the radio asking us what we'd got over there. We replied, "Standby", as we cleaned up with the rest of our bombs. Then, before we left, we read off the coordinates of the other targets remaining for the FAC(A) to work with. It was a good day – we cleaned off both jets twice in one day.'

The range of targets discovered and attacked is as holistic as it is impressive. The Strike Eagle is credited with destroying over 60 per cent of the estimated total force of the Iraqi Medina Republican Guard. It scored direct hits on more than 65 Iraqi MiGs on the ground, as well as hitting key IADS and C3I targets that often required crews to fly deep inside the Baghdad Super MEZ (Missile Exclusion Zone). Finally, the F-15E supported Coalition infantry and armour on the ground.

IRAQI ORDER OF BATTLE

The Baghdad Super MEZ was the euphemism for the SAM sites encircling the capital, which represented Iraq's thickest and most potent missile threat. The MEZ, which resembled the silhouette of Disney character 'Mickey Mouse's' head, comprised Roland, SA-2, SA-3, SA-6, SA-8, SA-9 and SA-13 missile systems, and at least one US-built I-Hawk SAM system from the occupation of Kuwait 12 years earlier. Of course, for each SAM system there was a multitude of AAA of all calibres up to 100 mm – Super MEZ indeed!

SCAR EXECUTION

Flying SCAR sorties worked out extremely well for the Strike Eagle. B-52s, B-1Bs, Navy F/A-18s and F-14s and Marine Corps AV-8Bs all used the F-15E to find, identify and hand-off targets to them, although there was extreme caution and more than a little consternation about the ramifications of inaccurate or poor PID and CDE in the war's early days.

In weapons system video tapes from the F-15E seen by the author, the two-person Strike Eagle crew is often heard working the radios hard. They show the WSO finding the target and talking the other platform on to it, with the pilot speaking to and controlling the positioning of other strike fighters as they enter the area. The cacophony of radio calls has to be heard to be believed. One can only imagine the strain that these crews were under, particularly when the final responsibility for PID and CDE fell to them. Capt Burbach said;

'Usually we talked to AWACS to get into the area, and after that we had little contact with them. Once in the kill box, we were assigned to

Platforms unable to conduct their own PID and CDE, such as this JDAM-equipped B-52H refuelling over the Indian Ocean, relied heavily on the F-15E to find and pass on targets which conformed to the OIF ROE (*USAF*)

SCAR, '1 Bravo' (the lead WSO) checking other flights into the area and '2 Bravo' (No 2's WSO) looking for targets. '2 Alpha' (No 2's pilot) would be flying mutual support because both guys in the lead jet had their heads in the cockpit. With the targets sorted, '1 Alpha' would cycle guys into the specific area and '1 Bravo' would talk '2 Bravo' onto the targets he wanted hit. If '2 Bravo' found something, then he would pass the target to us and take on the responsibility of talking our eyes onto the target. We passed lots of FDL data to one another to make sure that we could kill targets quickly and concisely. The front-seaters would keep an eye out for threats once we were ready to drop our bombs.'

There were often complications when working with other assets, particularly those which had no onboard PID capabilities, as Capt Meziere pointed out;

'There were some PID and CDE issues for SCAR. I would have comm with my wingman on the auxiliary radio to allow us to talk each other's eyes on to the target, but a few days into the war it became obvious there was actually very little talking between us at all. Working with the B-52s and B-1s was different, though. They couldn't perform their own PID and CDE, so when they said to us, "Hey, we got some bombs. Just tell us where to put them", we would respond, "Well, do you have your own PID and CDE?"' They did not, of course, and the Strike Eagle crews were justified in refusing to give them drop coordinates.

The CAOC eventually cleared the Strike Eagle to perform PID and CDE on behalf of the B-52, but neither Meziere or Burbach can recall ever giving clearance for B-52s or B-1s to drop on their targets for the duration of the war. F-15E crews were expected to assume 100 per cent accountability for any bomb dropped under their own PID and CDE calls. Their reluctance to clear a 'blind' platform (*text continues on page 62*)

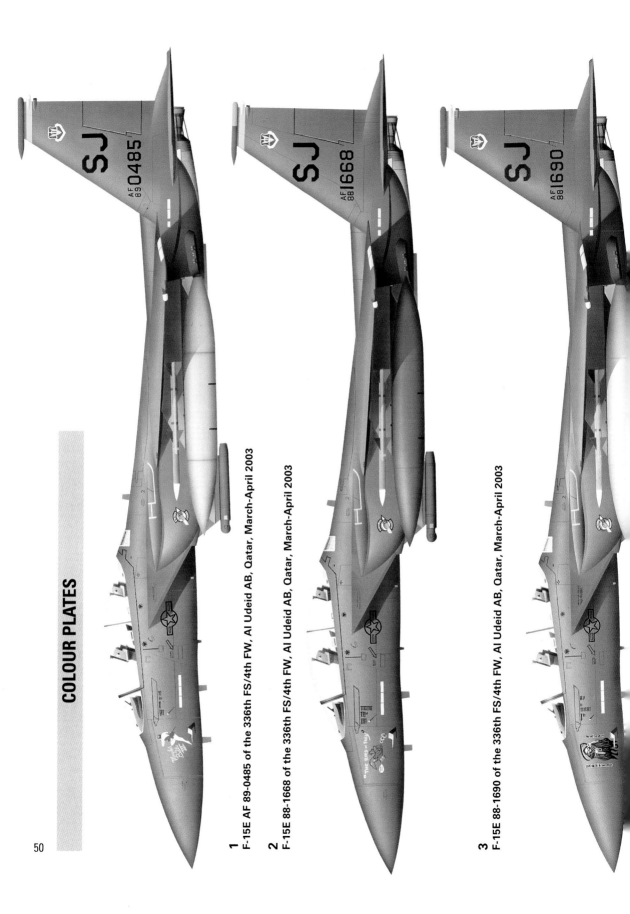

COLOUR PLATES

1
F-15E AF 89-0485 of the 336th FS/4th FW, Al Udeid AB, Qatar, March–April 2003

2
F-15E 88-1668 of the 336th FS/4th FW, Al Udeid AB, Qatar, March–April 2003

3
F-15E 88-1690 of the 336th FS/4th FW, Al Udeid AB, Qatar, March–April 2003

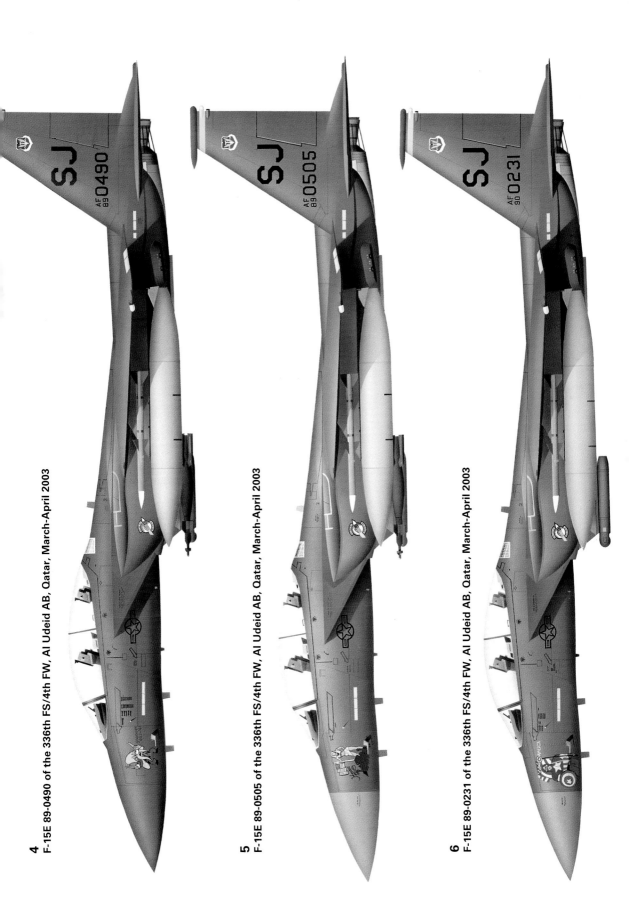

4
F-15E 89-0490 of the 336th FS/4th FW, Al Udeid AB, Qatar, March–April 2003

5
F-15E 89-0505 of the 336th FS/4th FW, Al Udeid AB, Qatar, March–April 2003

6
F-15E 89-0231 of the 336th FS/4th FW, Al Udeid AB, Qatar, March–April 2003

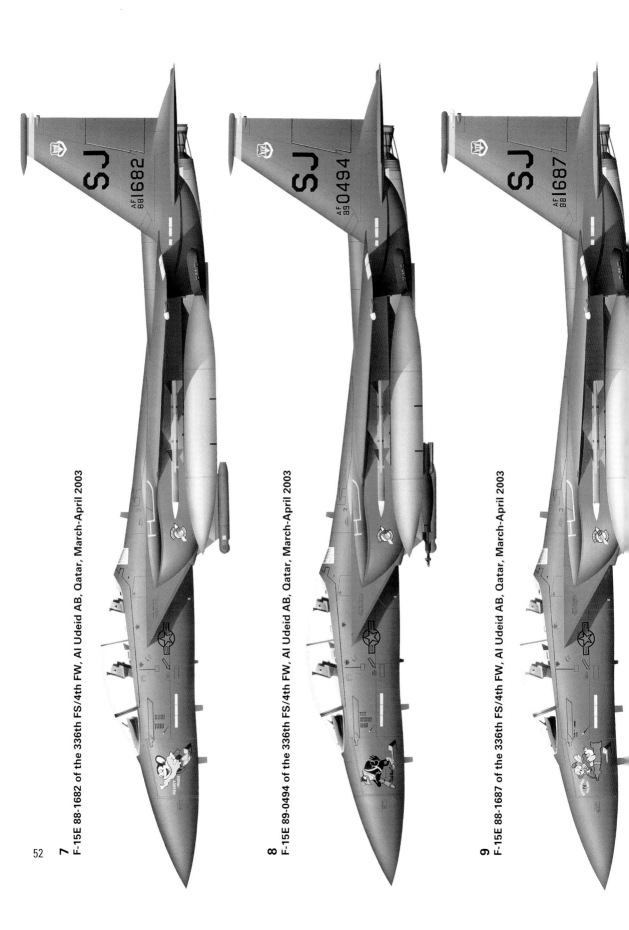

52

7
F-15E 88-1682 of the 336th FS/4th FW, Al Udeid AB, Qatar, March-April 2003

8
F-15E 89-0494 of the 336th FS/4th FW, Al Udeid AB, Qatar, March-April 2003

9
F-15E 88-1687 of the 336th FS/4th FW, Al Udeid AB, Qatar, March-April 2003

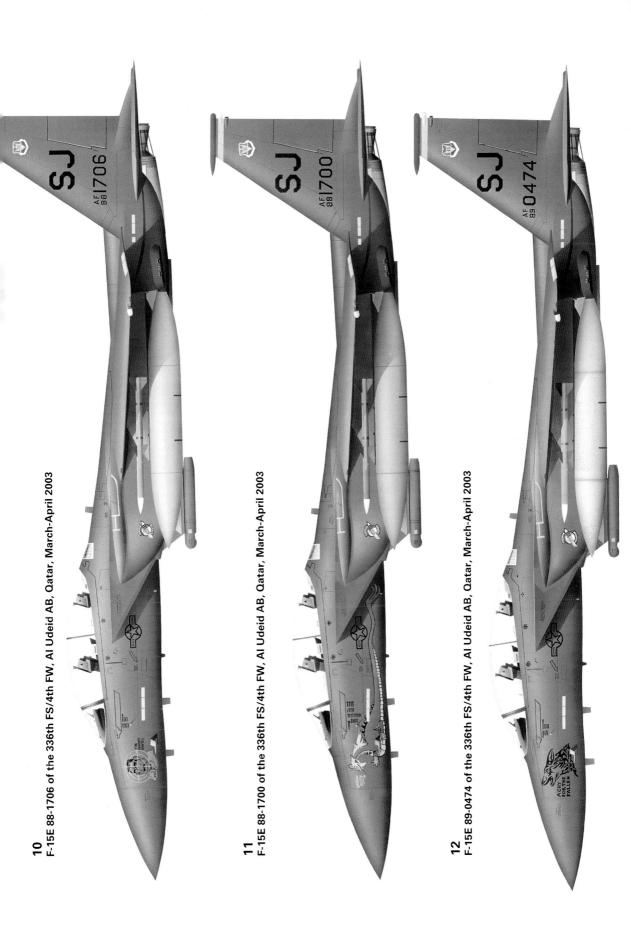

10
F-15E 88-1706 of the 336th FS/4th FW, Al Udeid AB, Qatar, March–April 2003

11
F-15E 88-1700 of the 336th FS/4th FW, Al Udeid AB, Qatar, March–April 2003

12
F-15E 89-0474 of the 336th FS/4th FW, Al Udeid AB, Qatar, March–April 2003

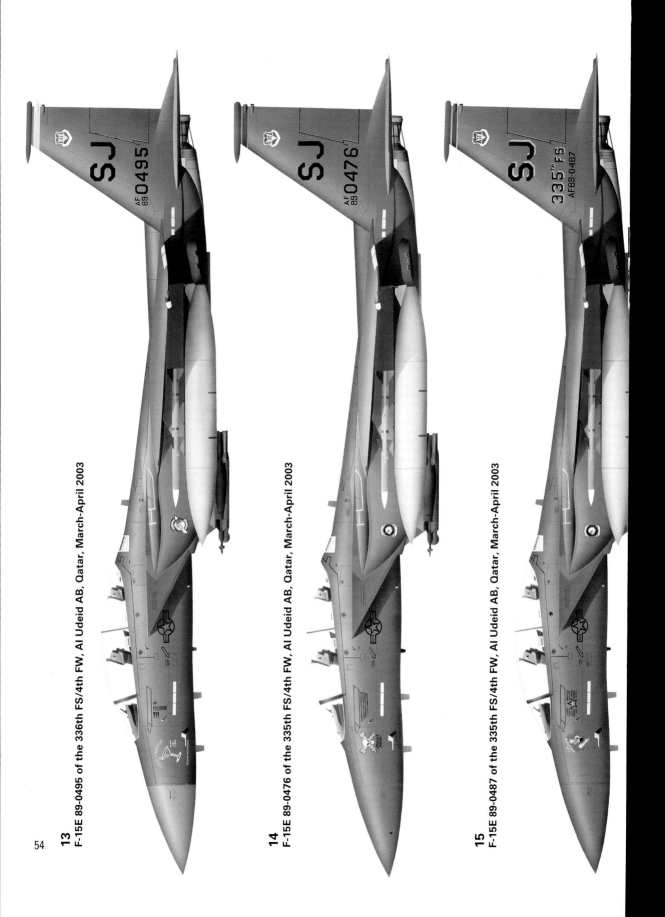

54

13
F-15E 89-0495 of the 336th FS/4th FW, Al Udeid AB, Qatar, March-April 2003

14
F-15E 89-0476 of the 335th FS/4th FW, Al Udeid AB, Qatar, March-April 2003

15
F-15E 89-0487 of the 335th FS/4th FW, Al Udeid AB, Qatar, March-April 2003

16
F-15E 89-0493 of the 335th FS/4th FW, Al Udeid AB, Qatar, March-April 2003

17
F-15E 88-1683 of the 335th FS/4th FW, Al Udeid AB, Qatar, March-April 2003

18
F-15E 89-0483 of the 335th FS/4th FW, Al Udeid AB, Qatar, March-April 2003

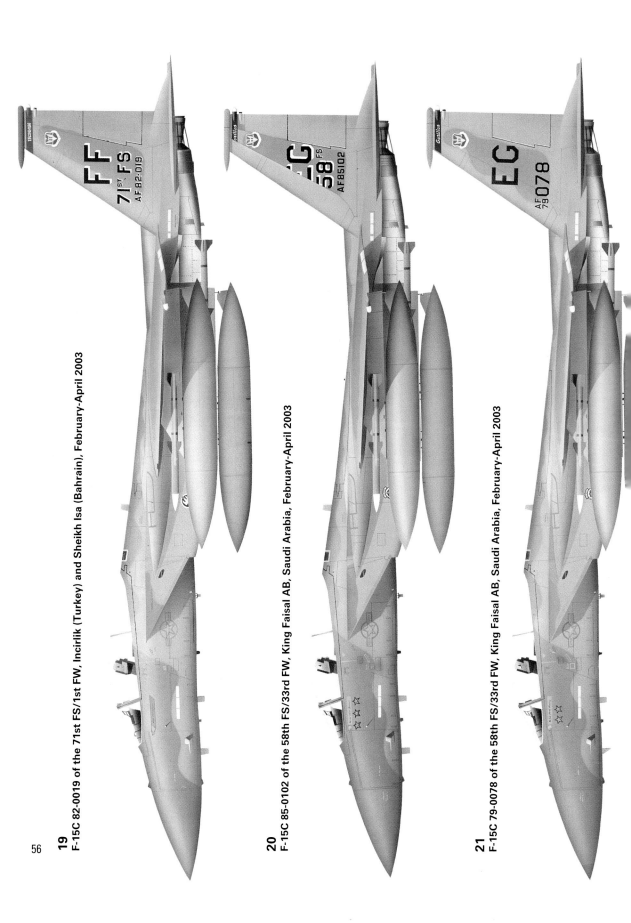

19
F-15C 82-0019 of the 71st FS/1st FW, Incirlik (Turkey) and Sheikh Isa (Bahrain), February-April 2003

20
F-15C 85-0102 of the 58th FS/33rd FW, King Faisal AB, Saudi Arabia, February-April 2003

21
F-15C 79-0078 of the 58th FS/33rd FW, King Faisal AB, Saudi Arabia, February-April 2003

Colour Nose Art Gallery

1
F-15E 88-1700 of the 336th FS/4th FW (*All nose art photographs by Randall Haskins via the author*)

2
F-15E 88-1687 of the 336th FS/4th FW

3
F-15E 88-1671 of the 336th FS/4th FW

4
F-15E ? of the 335th FS/4th FW

5
F-15E 89-0493 of the 335th FS/4th FW

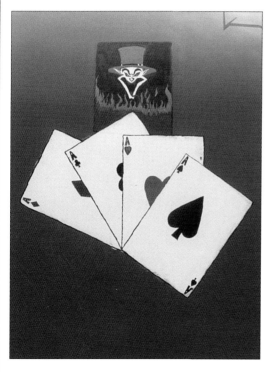

6
F-15E 88-1683 of the 335th FS/4th FW

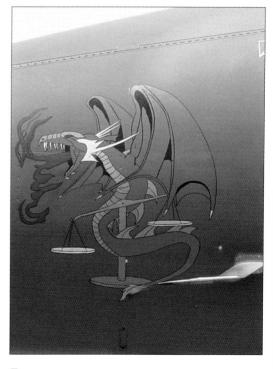

7
F-15E 88-1672 of the 336th FS/4th FW

8
F-15E 90-0231 of the 336th FS/4th FW

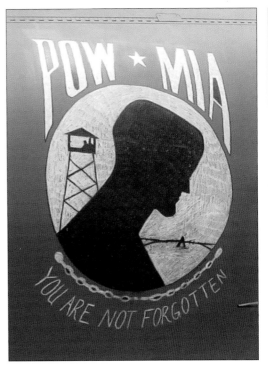

9
F-15E 88-1686 of the 335th FS/4th FW

10
F-15E 88-1668 of the 336th FS/4th FW

11
F-15E 89-0485 of the 336th FS/4th FW

12
F-15E 89-0474 of the 336th FS/
4th FW

13
F-15E 88-1706 of the 336th FS/4th FW

14
F-15E 88-1682 of the 336th FS/4th FW

15
F-15E 88-1675 of the 336th FS/4th FW

16
F-15E 89-0494 of the 336th FS/4th FW

17
F-15E 89-0505 of the 336th FS/4th FW

18
F-15E 87-0195 of the 336th FS/4th FW

19
F-15E 89-0490 of the 336th FS/4th FW

to drop is therefore understandable. Capt Burbach summarised the situation in the following quote;

'We're always taught that if there is a doubt, there is no doubt. We had some issues with the way we passed coordinates to the B-52s, and we asked ourselves if they were going to be good enough to put a JDAM on. Such concerns remained with us throughout OIF.'

The Army Ground Liaison Officers (GLOs), of whom there were ten at Al Udeid, became more and more useful to the Strike Eagle community as time moved on. In the beginning there was a lack of appreciation of the mechanics of each other's roles. The Strike Eagle community was unsure about the best way to extract pertinent information from the GLOs, who were in turn unsure of what the F-15E crews needed to know. Burbach;

'To begin with there would be times when we'd come back with all our bombs. We'd say to ourselves, "This is ridiculous. There are so many targets out there that someone must know where they all are". In the end, we just started asking more, and better, questions.'

The wing's F-15E aircrew rapidly benefited from a better understanding of the ground war's overall impetus and objectives. The productivity of the relationship between the GLO and aircrew soon soared. Coordination with regular Army and Marine ground forces was also assisted by the presence of at last three Strike Eagle aircrew embedded with forward ground units as G-FACs (Ground-FACs). They were used to call in air strikes and to coordinate other aerial support when necessary. For the crews of the 'Chiefs' and 'Rocketeers', it became something of a novelty to be able to radio a ex-squadronmate while on the way back from a sortie for an impromptu chat.

Before departing on a sortie, the WSO and pilot would discuss the locations their SCAR mission would take them over. Intelligence would provide a list of targets within those kill boxes, and would also provide 'dump targets' when possible. There was a hierarchy of targets onto which the Strike Eagle was tasked to drop – tanks, armoured personnel carriers, infantry and heavy weaponry – but in the event that they were unable to find any, the dump targets would be used as an alternative.

THIRTY MINUTES OVER KIRKUK

In late March the F-15E was tasked to fly KI missions near Baghdad itself. Vicious sand storms and poor weather had forced the Strike Eagles further north in search of suitable targets not obscured by cloud or flying sand, as these could be struck more readily. Capt Joe Siberski remembered one particular sortie during this period;

'We were flying KI missions, and we'd go to these places to try and find targets, but if the weather was too bad they'd move us along to try and find a better area to work in. At this point in time the Army had still not moved much because the sandstorms had really slowed their progress. On this day we were supposed to go right over Baghdad, but we found there was bad weather over the city and there was no way we could do any work there. We descended to what we thought was a comfortable height, but we found ourselves still very much in the weather. We were thinking there's no way this'll work, so as we climbed back up, "Cowboy" (pilot) said to me, "Well, what do you say we go and see where this weather ends?"

Several airfields north of Baghdad had not been visited since they were attacked during Operation *Desert Storm* in 1991. Some 12 years later during OIF, US Special Forces as well as regular troops parachuted into a number of them when an overland invasion via Turkey was forbidden by the Turkish government (*Gary Klett via author*)

'We started flying north, figuring out how much gas we had and exactly how far we could go before we had to turn around and go meet our next tanker slot. As we headed north, we were high so as to save gas and improve our general visibility.

'I looked at the TSD (Tactical Situation Display – moving map), and sure enough I could see Kirkuk. As we got there the weather ended, and we could see the civilian airfield, the town and the military airfield. We dropped down to where LAN-TIRN could look around, and saw the military airfield with a whole load of revetments spread about. It was neat because the clouds had just moved through there, revealing this sleepy little town. I said to "Cowboy", "You know I have never flown *Northern Watch* before and I've never seen the landscape up here (north of Baghdad). It's a lot different up here than down south". He replied, "Hey buddy, this is what ONW looks like". The big difference was that Kirkuk was actually *south* of the northern no-fly zone, so no one had gone there since 1991. Indeed, "Cowboy" said, "The last time anyone was here was *Desert Storm*".

'We flew around a little longer and took a look at the military airfield, doing a little bit of pod recce to see what we could see. The revetments were full of military vehicles, and we could see ammo caches and things like that. We decide to call up the AWACS that was up north. We basically had to wake this guy up. He dropped his coffee cup and was asking, "Who's this?" There was no one flying out of Turkey, and he was just not expecting any one from the south to be operating that far north. We knew that lots of people were coming back with full loads of bombs because of the weather, but we thought we may as well do something, so we asked the AWACS to call back to the CAOC and tell them that we were going back to the tanker for gas. The winds were good, and we wanted to loiter over Kirkuk and kill the military stuff on the airfield. We were thinking, "It looks like these people below us don't even know a war's going on. Maybe we'd better tell them!"

'The northern AWACS called "Dad" (CAOC), and as we got out of radio range from the northern AWACS and got on the tanker, we asked the southern AWACS to give us a radio relay and call the northern AWACS to see what the CAOC was saying. As we were getting our gas, the word came back. Sure enough, the boss had cleared us to strike any military vehicle or target that fell within the perimeter of the base. We were like, "Hoooly cow! Here we go, buddy!"

'We cruised back up north, right over Baghdad in the weather. This was when we realised that their SAM threat was ineffective if you stayed at high altitude, so we gave them the "finger" as we passed overhead. The clouds had now crept in a little bit, and so we descended to make sure that we knew what we're hitting. We knew there were no friendlies there, but we descended anyway.

'The funny thing was that the first time we were there, as we were leaving, I thought I saw something out of the corner of my eye. I thought that our No 2 had dropped a flare, so I didn't take much notice of it. But now we were back again, and as I thought about it again, I realise they'd taken a pot shot at us as we'd left to get gas.

We quickly sorted our targeting between the two WSOs, and I told "2B" to take anything south of a large structure in the middle of the airfield. I was going to take everything north of it. We proceeded to run and drop our first bombs, and as soon as they hit – "Oh My God!" The Iraqis decided that today was the day they were going to shoot every 57 mm AAA round they had. We were actually above it for the most part, and I think that they fired all that ammunition in the expectation that we were going to come in lower. It was not really a factor, but it was impressive.

'I was now hoping that we could hit some of that AAA because that was the kind of stuff we needed to take out if we were to bring people in there eventually. On our third target run they shoot a Roland at us, and that really got my attention. "Cowboy" and I saw it at the same time. "Cowboy", being the experienced aviator he is, had no hesitation at all. The next thing I knew my face was buried in my lap and we had lots of G on the jet. In peace-time, we always practice our threat calls and they sound cool, but when the "rubber hits the road" all I got out was "mrph, mrph, mrph" as I tried to make the threat call with the G forces burying my head into my lap. It was definitely not your John Wayne style of threat call!

'At that point we still had a bomb in flight with less than five seconds to impact. We just hoped it hit something close to the aiming point. We knew that the Roland was a fast missile, and that it had a short time of flight, so "Cowboy" came out of the break turn and immediately pulled into where we thought it should be. And there it was, exploding behind us, some distance away. As I was "cleaning out my drawers", and we were pushing away from the threat area, we decided to get above the Roland envelope. I asked "Cowboy", "Do you think it's a good idea to go back with our last remaining bomb?" He replied, "Are you kidding me? Of course we have to go back!"

'Of course, he was right. We finished off the rest of our bombs from higher altitude and then left our disposable fuel tanks on the outskirts of

Taking on fuel from a 9th Air Refueling Squadron/60th Air Mobility Wing KC-10A tanker before returning north to continue a KI/CAS mission, this 336th jet is seen flying over southern Iraq towards the end of March 2003. The four KC-10 units in-theatre were all specially formed expeditionary squadrons created for OIF. They used aircraft drawn from regular frontline wings, however, hence the markings on this example from Travis AFB, California (*Randall Haskin via author*)

Kirkuk as we headed back south. As we left the city, I saw a AAA piece firing away at us. It was right in the middle of a housing development, well away from the airfield.

This was the day that we had brought the war to Kirkuk. We were pretty satisfied with that. Those guys (Iraqis) up there thought they were going to get away with it when Turkey refused to let us operate from Incirlik. They were wrong.'

MOVING TARGETS

From the first night of hostilities, the 'Chiefs' and the 'Rocketeers' flew

The 500-lb bomb body of a GBU-12 LGB awaits the fitment of its nose guidance section at the load barn at RAF Lakenheath. This example, which is an inert training round, has had both its rear guidance fins and nose collar installed (*author/FJ Photography.com*)

KI/CAS and SCAR missions against both fixed and moving-targets. While killing fixed targets with LGBs – usually GBU-10s and GBU-12s – proved simple enough in most cases, it was the mobile targets which presented the greatest challenge. The F-15E, however, excelled at striking them, even if they were travelling in random directions or simply at high-speed along one of the many highways branching out from Baghdad. Once again, OEF had been the proving ground for the Strike Eagle, and the crews from the 4th FW were mentally prepared for the task at hand.

Hitting a moving target with a 500-lb GBU-12 was not dissimilar in theory to clay pigeon shooting with a shotgun. The WSO would gauge the relative motion and direction of the vehicle and then point his laser a set distance ahead of it. By generating this lead, the bomb would be released with enough energy to strike the target as it continued to travel. With the bomb in flight, the laser would be fired some eight to ten seconds before impact and the weapon would guide onto the laser spot. If the WSO had been too generous with the lead he could massage the laser spot back towards the vehicle, causing the LGB to sharpen its trajectory.

Conversely, the bomb could be dragged further by adding lead to the vehicle if necessary. With the TIMPACT (time to impact) counter in the

An armourer checks the loading of a GBU-12 with a new MAU-169J/B seeker head at Al Udeid . Capt Joe Siberski summarised the improvements to the bomb's accuracy with these new seekers when he said, 'it's like driving nails' (*USAF*)

jet counting down, the WSO could gradually bring the laser spot onto the vehicle itself. With any luck it would allow the bomb to score a direct hit. This technique was used not just from ahead and behind target vehicles, but also at acute angles from their direction of travel. 'The video of hitting moving trucks with GBU-12s from 90 degrees of heading difference is eye-watering', Capt Haskin added.

Sometimes the driver was well prepared for the impending attack, and it then became necessary to force him to react by placing a

bomb in front of him, predicting the vehicle would turn left (for example) if the impact was slightly to its right. With the plan confirmed, No 2 could release his bomb just as lead's bomb impacted the ground. With luck, the vehicle would turn in the predicted direction and No 2's weapon was already well on its way. Similar tactics could be used when a string of dumb bombs were dropped in the path of an oncoming column, or when the head and tail of the column were struck first. This forced the rest to act predictably by leaving the road and trying to scatter along unprepared terrain. There was the added benefit of slowing the targets down.

Within a few weeks of the commencement of OIF, the F-15E squadrons started to receive the new MAU-169J/B seeker head for their 500-lb GBU-12 LGBs. Capt Siberski immediately noticed the difference between the old and new seekers, as he explained;

'They were improved seekers that came out when we started getting through the GBU-12 stocks. I noticed a much better guide with the new seekers, and so did a couple of other guys. It was like driving nails with those things. They were transparent to the user, for we dropped the bomb as normal . . . just more precisely.'

The 'Rocketeers' and 'Chiefs' went through GBU-12s at such a prodigious rate that they used up all the new seekers and eventually had to revert back to the older ones. With the capability to carry nine GBU-12s per aircraft, a two-ship of Strike Eagles could pack a devastating punch against as many as 18 individual targets. The 500-lb LGB was the F-15Es' staple munition, deployed in larger numbers than the similar sized, and much-vaunted, GBU-31 JDAM.

LITENING II APPRAISAL

The few serviceable AAQ-28s were providing some great daytime PID capabilities according to Capt Siberski, but they also had poor night-time (infra-red sensor) characteristics;

'The pod made life a lot easier for me for almost one reason alone – positive target identification. The only way to ID something like a vehicle with the LANTIRN pod (AAQ-14) was to fly your precious ass into the heart of every single threat the bad guy has – not a good way to do business. With the Litening pod, we could stay at medium altitude and ID from there. Now, that sounds like a huge upgrade in capability for the Strike Eagle because our Pilot/WSO coordination and software integration makes for a lethal combination from medium altitude. But there's more.

It's a huge capability boost for *all* war fighters. With a Litening II pod, we can ID and hand off targets to any platform over the radio, and we can also hand them off digitally to other data link capable systems, which is best.'

But Siberski added that the pod also demonstrated some inferior characteristics. As he put it;

'I couldn't stand the Litening in IR mode once stuff started burning. The AAQ-28 uses a different part of the IR spectrum to the LANTIRN. I'm told the different spectrum allows the pod to be more sensitive, hence the much better picture. My observation is that this spectrum is more sensitive to washing out the picture when secondary explosions are going off in the area of interest. Furthermore, the Litening II was originally

Litening II's main advantages were the quality of its EO sensor and the laser spot tracker that could 'follow' the coded laser pulse from another aircraft's own designator. But its infra-red sensor was prone to thermal blooming (as seen in the photograph immediately below), making it less useful at night (*USAF and author/FJ Photography. com*)

engineered for F-16s (single-seat mentality), and there was little "manual tuning" ability like there is for LANTIRN. Instead, there was a range of tuning settings, called histograms, that we could step through.

'The guys at the 422nd TES (Test & Evaluation Squadron) spent a lot of time trying to tweak the different histograms to deal with blooming, but I still had issues. I did most of my flying with it during the day, so I usually had the EO camera selected. The EO camera is superb in good visibility, and the only blooming you have to worry about is the dirt, fire and target parts covering your next target.'

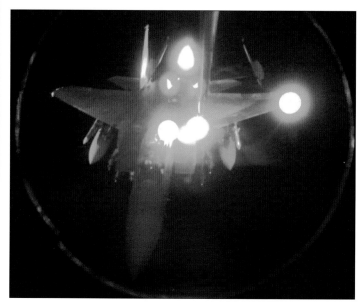

Capt Burbach had some very positive experiences with the AAQ-28's spot tracker, as he explained;

'We worked with some of the FAC(A) F-14A guys who were at the Deid. On one occasion the Tomcat RIO (Radar Intercept Officer) said to me, "Okay, here's my laser code, I'm lasing now". He lased a DMPI (desired mean point of impact – target) and said, "Here's the first one". Then he dragged my laser spot tracker over to the next target and said, "Here's the second one". He dragged it over to the third one. I made a mark point on the first, gave my wingman the second DMPI and we dropped on the same run-in and hit both targets simulta-

neously. Then we turned around and dropped on the third target, with the F-14A lasing my bomb in for me.'

This kind of utility is valuable – just as FDL is – and the expertise and professionalism of the Tomcat FAC(A)s allowed Strike Eagle aircrew who worked with them to get the most out of their new pods. While not typical of most F-15E crews' experience in OIF, this mission nevertheless showed what was possible when conditions allowed.

ROLAND LAUNCH

Despite the dilapidated state of the Iraqi IADS, and the battlefield preparations carried out by Coalition aircraft during OSW, the mobile SAM threat remained very real for the first few weeks of the conflict. Capt Haskin recorded his experiences of an encounter with a Roland SAM on 31 March in the following detailed diary entry;

'Somewhere out there in central Iraq tonight there is a Roland SAM operator who's talking about "the one that got away". Today, I was No 2 of "Junker 67" flight, and we were "fragged" to drop GBU-12s in the kill box right over downtown Baghdad. Initially we flew into Al Jaber, in Kuwait, where we hot pitted and topped off the tanks. Then we were off to central Iraq. Unfortunately, the weather was bad everywhere in Iraq. There were clouds from about 14,000 ft all the way up to above 25,000 ft right in the prime piece of airspace where we wanted to work. Below, there were more broken decks of clouds, as well as thick haze and poor visibility.

'After checking in with the AWACS (call-sign "Luger"), we were given a number of targets that they wanted us to drop on. J-STARS even had some movers for us to investigate, but going below a 14,000-ft ceiling in central Baghdad is a death wish because it would be easy for AAA gunners to spot us flying under the overcast. We burned our first load of gas just trying to find workable airspace, and eventually had to go back and top off from a KC-135 in the "Scratchy Central" tanker track.

'After topping off – and still with our full load of nine GBUs – we knew we'd have to try to find work somewhere else. Three times we received tasking to investigate and bomb targets in the kill boxes just south of Baghdad. Weather continued to be poor, so each time we poked our nose into the area we found the cloud cover completely obscuring it, forcing us to abort our tasking. Finally, getting low on fuel, we accepted one last tasking from "Warhawk" to investigate and kill a convoy of armoured vehicles in a compound near a main highway some 40 miles south of Baghdad near Iskandiriyah and Karbala. This is also the area in which two Apaches were shot down last week.

'We found a hole in the clouds and descended through the undercast. Once we got below 14,000 ft, we found that the visibility was absolutely lousy – probably four or five miles at best in haze. On our first pass through the target area we couldn't identify a single hostile vehicle. My WSO was working his ass off, but the targeting pod visibility was terrible. I was working hard, too, because I could barely see a thing outside. It was so tough just keeping my lead in sight that I had to perform a radar lock on him intermittently.

'We made a big sweeping counter-clockwise turn to the east of the tar-get area, then looped around to make another north-to-south sweep

Capt Randall Haskin captured this shot of his WSO deep in thought as they returned home from the mission described in the text. Roland missiles popped up frequently during OIF, and Haskin and his WSO were among several crews to have found themselves on the wrong end of one of these deadly French-built SAMs (*Randall Haskin via author*)

through. Being down low, I was very vigilant about moving the aeroplane, randomly making heading and altitude changes, and keeping my eyes outside looking for AAA fire. We hadn't seen much AAA yet, but as we approached the target, two white airbursts appeared about 500 ft off my right wingtip.

'I jammed a quick turn away from the puffs and kept my eyes out for more airbursts. Fortunately none appeared. One thing I noticed as I was making hard turns was that the moisture in the air was creating some very visible streamers off my wingtips. While I'm sure that would have looked mighty cool in peacetime, now the "vapes" were highlighting me to anyone on the ground who bothered to look – not exactly what you want when the guys on the ground are shooting back at you!

'On this second pass over the target area, "Maddog" was able to see the area where the vehicles were parked more clearly through the pod. While he could make out vehicles, he couldn't positively identify them enough to drop a bomb. With gas running low, we were going to try one more pass through the area and attempt to drop our bombs. We continued our counterclockwise flow, this time ingressing the target at 13,000 ft from the east to the west.

'This time "Maddog" had a good target designation, and was still working hard to identify vehicles through the murky LANTIRN picture. As the TREL time ticked down I was anticipating hearing the "captured, cleared to release" call, but it was pretty damn quiet from the back seat. At five TREL, and still with no "captured" call from the back, it was evident that it just wasn't going to happen.

'So it was time to go home, with a full load of bombs still on the jet. What a waste to have flown 600 miles, deep into Iraq and have to take those bombs all the way back home just because of bad weather!

'I banked hard left and started to egress the target area to the south. My flight lead was about two miles in front of me, already climbing up to conserve fuel on the way home. I had barely finished my turn when I heard the RWR (radar warning receiver) wailing in my headset. I was used to hearing the steady "nails" tone from the RWR that was constantly going off in response to the radars of the hundreds of fighter aircraft operating over Iraq. To be quite honest, I'd almost gotten so used to hearing it that I wasn't being disciplined about looking at the RWR every time I heard the tone, then verbalising what it was so that my WSO would know, too. This tone, however, was one I hadn't heard yet during OIF – the missile launch tone!

'Before I looked at the RWR itself, my eyes cued in on the bright red warning light on the instrument panel, located just below the glareshield at eye level. It said "SAM". At the same time "Maddog" shouted through the intercom, "ROLAND". My eyes darted to the symbol on the RWR that indicated that we were being shot at by a Roland short-range SAM.

'What was strange was that the RWR was telling me I was right on top of the SAM site. That wasn't a situation we had really trained for back at Seymour Johnson, so I knew I had to get my eyeballs on the missile ASAP.

'My first move was to plug in maximum afterburner and make a hard turn 30 degrees to the right, dumping out two bursts of chaff, then another hard jink 45 degrees back to the left. At this point I was still at just under 400 knots – a good fighting airspeed – so I pulled the throttles back out of blower. I didn't want to present an overly ripe heat signature, since at 13,000 ft I was also in a WEZ for several IR-guided SAMs. I looked over my left shoulder and down the wing line at the target area, trying to visually acquire the missile in flight. Since the Roland is very fast, I knew I only had seconds to locate the missile and outmanoeuvre it. Unfortunately, I saw nothing. With the missile site most likely having been at my "low six o'clock" position, the fuselage and wings would have been blocking my line of sight regardless of how much I was turning and jinking.

'My initial defensive moves out of the way, it was time to tell "Junker 1" that I was getting shot at. Many times on this trip I've run into occasions where my training kicked in and I just reacted to circumstances without thinking about it. This, however, was not one of them! If it were a training sortie where we were practicing SAM threat reactions, I'd have said "'Junker 2's' defending south. Mud Roland". Instead, I simply blurted out – yelled, practically – "One Roland launch!" with my Bullseye location, followed by "I don't see the missile!" over the intercom. "Maddog" was maintaining his composure much better than I was, saying simply "I don't see the missile", while twisting himself up like a pretzel in the back seat trying to turn around and see it.

'After two more hard turns, many more chaff actuations and even a few flares dropped, the Roland indication left my RWR scope. "Two's naked", I said, and began to let out a sigh of relief that we were still flying and, apparently, had either not been launched on or evaded the missile.

'Almost as quickly as it had gone away, the Roland symbol flashed on my scope again, this time at my very close "six o'clock". The missile launch tone also returned to my headset. I continued pumping out chaff and modified my manoeuvring. Although the electronics were telling me that there was a missile in the air, neither of us could see one.

'"Maddog" and I were going through the same thought processes, evidently, because as my left arm moved off the throttles and toward the combat jettison button on the lower left instrument panel, he commented, "Think about the tank". Dropping the external fuel tanks lightens the aeroplane's weight, reduces drag and improves manoeuvrability – all things that I want while I'm fighting a missile shot at me. With my left index finger I punched the red button once, and with a satisfying little "clunk", much like the feeling when a 500-lb bomb is dropped, the tanks fell away from the wing stations. Looking back to my "six o'clock', and with the jet in a hard right 90-degree bank, I saw the light grey tanks bobbling end-over-end through the air as they dropped away.

'More chaff and hard manoeuvring followed, and eventually my RWR went quiet. I was still frantically looking for the missiles, but I never saw them. My flight lead after the sortie commented that he watched both

A French-built Roland is fired from its launcher. Vast numbers of these highly effective SAMs were supplied to Iraq throughout the 1980s, and they posed the greatest threat to Coalition aircraft in OIF

missiles zip up toward us from below, leaving two white smoke trails, then detonate on chaff less than a mile behind us.

'I can't help taking being shot at personally. Many times, flying aeroplanes and dropping bombs seems a very impersonal way to fight. This time, however, it feels like it was *mano-e-mano* – me versus the SAM operator – and I won. It's just too bad that I couldn't go back and cram a "500-pounder" down his throat as a going away present to the loser of the fight – I was too low on fuel!'

Cockpit Voice Recording Transcript of the Roland Incident

2A = Capt Haskin (pilot)
2B = Capt Farrell (WSO)
1A = Flight lead (pilot)
2A: *Five* (seconds to bomb drop)
2B: *Negative* (WSO cannot capture target in TP)
2A: *Okay*
(RWR Launch Tone)
2B: *Roland!*
2A: (Under G) *Chaff, Chaff*
2B: (Grunting) *I didn't see the missile*
2A: (UHF2) *One, Roland launch, bullseye . . .*
2B: *Chaff*
2A: (UHF2) *. . . 161 for 80*
2A: (UHF2) *I don't see the missile*
2B: *I didn't see it, either*
2A: (UHF2) *Two's naked* (No RWR indications)
(RWR Launch Tone)
2B: *Roland launch*
2A: (UHF2, under G) *Two's Roland launch, still 162 for 82, BRA 030*
2B: (Under G) *Think about the tanks . . .*
2A: (Still under G) *Jett! Tanks are gone*
A: (UHF2) *Two's naked*
1A: (UHF2) *One's naked*
2B: *Dude, I'm tempted to go back there and f***in' kill 'em!*
2A: *No way, man!*
2B: (Laughing) *Ya big p***y!*

SPECIAL FORCES

The Special Forces (SF) operation in Iraq, which was given the innocuous-sounding name Task Force *Tawny*, began long before OIF. Once the war was in full swing, it was the 335th FS which provided the bulk of their airborne support, with the 336th FS also contributing from time to time.

The most sensitive of these so-called 'TF-20' lines were the dedicated SF support sorties flown by a handful of 335th aircrew – only ten pilots and WSOs were 'read-in' on them – and these missions were heavily compartmentalised in terms of mission planning and briefing/debriefing. TF-20 aircrews were given a free hand to plan their sorties, together with securing the assets and weapons needed to get the job done. The author understands that AAQ-28 pods and GBU-24 LGBs were used extensively by these crews – 24 GBU-24s were dropped by the F-15E during the course of the war.

These highly-classified missions usually involved loitering within a 'black' kill box and communicating with ground operators over secure KY-58 radios. The SF troops usually carried covert IR strobes to allow the F-15E crews to acquire them visually using NVGs. Sometimes, they operated their own laser designators to allow 'buddy lasing' of the Strike Eagle's LGBs. More often, though, the operators on the ground would use a sophisticated laser rangefinder to provide ranging and ground coordinates for targets to strike. SF troops were most densely located in northern and western Iraq, where the 'Chiefs' spent most of their time.

For much of the war a BBC camera crew shadowed these men and filmed them calling in air strikes from F-15Es, F/A-18s and F-14s in northern Iraq. Indeed, a post-war BBC documentary showed the camera crew working side-by-side with US SF teams.

When conducting operations with SF, the eyes of the pilot or WSO were usually talked onto the target by the ground commander. Sometimes this proved much easier said than done. For example, on one occasion a team of soldiers (the interviewee who recounted the story referred to the ground forces in non-explicit terms – the author has deduced that there is a strong likelihood that these 'soldiers' were probably SF) had come under fire from a group of Fedayeen militiamen. On foot and unable to give chase, the ground commander told the circling F-15Es to 'find and attack a white Toyota Corolla with tinted windows'! This was an impossible task for the Strike Eagle crew, whose target pod simply could not discern such detail from the altitudes at which they were flying. With the soldiers on the ground in no immediate danger, the crew elected not to descend below the 10,000 ft minimum altitude imposed upon them by the wing.

When the situation demanded, however, some crews elected to descend as low as 7500 ft (into the MANPAD threat envelope) so as to PID the target. Once accomplished, the pilot would climb back up to the 'mid teens' to deploy ordnance. This was the preferred altitude for most weapon releases when supporting SF, as it offered a good compromise between safety and expedience.

When the situation became so precarious that a bomb could not be placed on a target without the risk of hitting a friendly soldier, the F-15E employed its M61A1 Vulcan cannon to good effect. On one video seen by the author, the SF commander could be heard saying, 'Good rounds. That's got 'em moving', as the 20 mm shells hit trees on the opposite side of the road from where he had taken refuge following an ambush. Despite several instances in OEF the year before, strafing was not an activity traditionally associated with the F-15E.

Individuals going through Strike Eagle training at Seymour Johnson

Only select 335th FS crews were cleared to fly the most sensitive of the SF missions, although crews from both 4th FW units participated in other SF support operations (*author/FJ Photography.com*)

had usually been told that 'Strike Eagles never strafe'. However, in OEF the 391st FS's F-15Es often used their guns against Taliban soldiers and vehicles threatening Coalition troops. Several months into the conflict in Afghanistan, the 335th FS also strafed extensively, and in the Battle for Roberts' Ridge (in which an attempt was made to recover the body of an SF operative) the gun was once again instrumental in protecting friendly ground forces. Those events provided the impetus to increase the frequency of gun training in the year that followed. Even then the leadership only considered the weapon an option for dire emergencies. Strike Eagle pilots were told that the M61A1 could only be employed if there were soldiers dying on the ground.

The author is aware of at least one instance in which a ground commander in Iraq asked for bullets and the F-15E flight lead gladly obliged, although he was later criticised by his seniors because it had not been a troops-in-contact, danger-close situation.

On other occasions, SF soldiers requested a show of force to try and flush out loyalist fighters. This required the Strike Eagles to fly highly-dangerous low passes right into the heart of the small arms envelope. Such passes were conducted down to 300 ft (at night), and usually required the pilot not only to fly directly over the enemy position, but also to dump flares to ward off the opposing forces.

These 'cloak and dagger' missions often involved direct contact with the operators on the ground, but there were instances when SF troops provided tip-offs via the CAOC or AWACS, resulting in Strike Eagles being re-tasked in-flight to kill time sensitive targets.

The four F-14A Tomcats from VF-154 (part of Carrier Air Wing Five embarked on the USS *Kitty Hawk* in the Northern Arabian Gulf) assigned to Al Udeid were there predominantly to assist with TF-20 missions. They left the base once the frequency of these sorties died down.

Of the few stories to surface about the SF work conducted by the 4th FW squadrons, perhaps the most interesting is the account of the overturned M1A1 Abrams tank which a regular Army unit had somehow managed to overturn while operating in the Tikrit region. Four 335th FS F-15Es had just left the area when a call came from an SF soldier who had been assigned to help recover the vehicle. Unarmed himself, his vehicle and fellow operators had come under heavy fire and he had fled on foot to find cover.

Cut-off from the main US unit, he and his men were desperately vulnerable and screaming on their radios for support as they ran at full speed away from the enemy. In the instant the call came through, all four F-15Es did a 180-degree turn and headed towards them. Once they located the SF soldier the crews attempted to pass him a heading for a nearby friendly unit, but under withering fire he and his troops were unable to move.

Simultaneously, AWACS called on two of the F-15Es to perform a TCT strike on a nearby airfield. Two of the four 'Chiefs' obliged and dropped GBU-12s, but with the weapons less than ten seconds from impact, their targets suddenly exploded. Unable to fathom out what had happened, the two returned to assisting the men on the ground. Eventually, the Strike Eagles gave cover and directions to a second group of soldiers who managed to find their way to the isolated SF operators.

Literally man-handling LGBs on the Al Udeid ramp, a veteran 335th FS 'ordie' gets to grips with rearming one of his charges in the warm spring sun. Aircraft supporting SF missions were given the first choice of all assets, resources and weapons needed to get the job done. These jets were often armed with the GBU-24, presumably because of its flexibility, but the more common, and smaller, GBU-10 and -12 were also popular (*USAF*)

It was during the flight debriefing that the FDL data was analysed to reveal a B-52 at 42,000 ft right on top of the Strike Eagles moments before the TCT targets had mysteriously exploded. It soon became apparent that this 'Buff', completely unaware of the fiasco unfolding directly below, had dropped a string of JDAMs right through the F-15E formation! This was not the first time that the Strike Eagles had come very close to being struck by bombs from aircraft not able to tap into the FDL network, for OEF had seen several instances of B-1s and B-52s dropping ordnance through formations of F-15Es.

The general feeling among the crews who witnessed this incident was that it was only a matter of time before a bomb hit a friendly aircraft. In their opinion, the sooner the B-52 and B-1 could be equipped with Link-16 to allow them to see where other friendlies were, the better.

Flying support for Special Operations usually required the F-15E pilot and WSO to override some of their keenest instincts. SF operators tried not to call the Strike Eagle into harm's way unless it was absolutely necessary, but on many occasions F-15Es descended right into the heart of SAM envelopes, including that of the much-feared Roland, to provide support. There was a tacit agreement between aircrew and soldiers that they would help each other out if either was being threatened. The tension in the voice of the man on the ground was usually enough to let the F-15E crew know when they had to throw away the rule book and do what was necessary to get the job done.

A story briefly discussed with the author recounted how SF soldiers had called an F-15E in to strike a position believed to be firing mortars at them. When the mortar rounds failed to fall nearby, the SF operator looked more closely at the offending site. 'Oh!' he radioed, 'I'm all right. He's actually firing 57 mm AAA at *you*!'.

SCUD HUNTING

Significant effort was invested in the anti-theatre ballistic missile mission by the 4th FW, particularly on the part of the OG. The employment of Weapons of Mass Destruction (WMD) was the Coalition's greatest fear pre-war, so preventing Saddam Hussein's forces from using them was a priority mission from the start of OIF. Dedicated sorties to police probable or suspected launch sites were placed at the top of the ATO.

The term 'Scud' is often applied to most forms of TBM, but there was actually a range of different missile systems which required neutralising should they be detected. Examples of the FROG-7A TBM and ABABIL 100 Al Fatah multiple launch rocket system were also known to be in the Iraqi arsenal, and both could prove deadly if allowed to operate freely. During these anti-

Searching for leadership and TBM targets often involved low-level passes over suspect vehicles. With eyes firmly out of the cockpit to scout for threats, the pilot would rely on the WSO to PID the target visually or through the pod (*Randall Haskin via author*)

missile patrols, the 'Rocketeers' destroyed several ABABIL and FROG launchers, as well as Scuds housed in fixed storage sites. One other system that gave cause for concern was the Chinese-built HY-2 'Seersucker' cruise missile. This weapon could be fired from a ground unit, and featured a warhead big enough to severely damage a 3000-ton warship. The 'Rocketeers' and 'Chiefs', therefore, flew anti-'Seersucker' patrols along the northern-Kuwaiti border, although it is not clear if any of these systems were actually discovered.

The hunt for mobile Scuds represented an interesting diversion from the constant flow of KI/CAS and SCAR missions. This was primarily because these sorties were usually conducted over western Iraq, and they saw crews operating over different areas of the country employing different techniques to locate them. Western Iraq was usually off-limits to the F-15E during OIF presumably because of the danger of jets inadvertently flying over Syria, and also due the presence of SF soldiers in the region.

Flying these missions fully-utilised the ground-moving target function of the radar, which could easily detect the cumbersome MAZ-543 launch vehicles against the backdrop of largely flat, rolling desert.

On one occasion, Capt Siberski located what he thought were two Scuds, but subsequent visual acquisition through his Litening II pod allowed him to determine that they were actually farmers' tractors towing flatbed trailers. Sensing the opportunity to have a little fun with a two-ship flight ahead of him equipped only with LANTIRN, he asked them to investigate, claiming he thought he had two Scuds but was unable to ID them. Of course, these two F-15E crews became excited for a short while as they attempted to locate and ID the vehicles with their inferior pods. The whole spectacle was a source of great amusement to Siberski and his two-ship element.

The only reported kills of the notorious MAZ-543 mobile SCUD launchers came on 2 April when two Strike Eagle crews were nominated for the Distinguished Flying Cross for their role in killing a Scud missile following a tip-off from SF soldiers on the ground. The F-15Es were

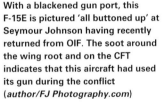

With a blackened gun port, this F-15E is pictured 'all buttoned up' at Seymour Johnson having recently returned from OIF. The soot around the wing root and on the CFT indicates that this aircraft had used its gun during the conflict (*author/FJ Photography.com*)

assigned to attack suspected MAZ-543 Al Hussein Scud launchers hidden in culverts under the main road running west from Baghdad to Al Quaim, on the Syrian border. 'Gundog 57' and '58' were given the TST from the CAOC with little time to plan. An impromptu 'buddy lasing' tactic was devised to destroy the ten assigned target areas while minimising collateral damage. The two aircraft took off and flew for approximately two hours to reach the AOR, completing one en route air-to-air refuelling.

AWACS advised 'Gundog' flight that there were friendly observers (almost certainly SF) within 1500 m of one of the targets, and the two fighters flew a trail/cover formation as the light faded, each taking it in turns to drop and lase. The improvised 'buddy lase' tactic required the lead jet to drop a GBU-12, while the trailing jet lased the bomb onto the target. The task was made more complex and dangerous by the orientation of each of the culverts, which necessitated an east-to-west attack axis, exposing the formation to AAA threats from Al Taqaddum airfield in the west and SAM threats from Baghdad in the east.

The first attack was successful. A GBU-12 dropped from 'Gundog 57' was guided by 'Gundog 58' into the southern-most culvert. 'Gundog 58' then assumed the in-flight tactical lead for the next drop. As 'Gundog 57' fell back to lase the bomb onto target, an SA-3 SAM became active to the east and heavy AAA fire appeared around the formation, including airbursts from 100 mm, 57mm and 37mm guns. As the pair flew east, and 'Gundog 58' released a single GBU-12 into the second culvert, the crew of the latter jet immediately witnessed a large smoke plume near their 'six o'clock' originating from Baghdad. Assessing it as a probable SA-3, 'Gundog 57' confirmed the missile launch over the radio. Both jets began aggressive defensive manoeuvring while maintaining target designation.

The second GBU-12 scored a direct hit, and due to the weapon's precise delivery and guidance secondary explosions were witnessed from the opposite side of the large culvert. Massive flames enveloped the western end, and these continued to burn for over an hour after the attack. SF observers later reported that this had indeed been the hiding location of an Al Hussein missile.

While no further SAM launches were encountered, AAA intensity increased with each subsequent attack. In addition, more SAMs in the Baghdad area started to come online. 'Gundog' made another buddy-guide delivery from west to east, but it became impossible to maintain the required formation position due to overwhelming AAA fire. With 'Gundog 58' physically separated from 'Gundog 57' by AAA airbursts, the two aircraft were no longer able to execute their 'buddy-lase' tactic.

Flight lead gave clearance for self-guided attacks, utilising alternating cover positions and remaining as far north as possible to avoid threats. Due to the orientation of the culvert openings, the next two attacks required flight paths over or near Baghdad. 'Gundog 57' executed two more self-guided GBU-12 attacks while 'Gundog 58' maintained constant awareness for the formation, calling out numerous AAA threats and directing the formation to minimise threat exposure while successfully attacking the culvert openings.

'Gundog' flight was credited with destroying one Scud SSM, as verified by the ground observers. Moreover, they had done so without causing any collateral damage despite the high risk of this occurring. The culverts were located under a major highway from Baghdad, and civilian traffic had actually continued along the highway for the duration of the attacks. But the fun was far from over.

Approaching a low fuel state, 'Gundog 58' requested two reconnaissance passes over Al Taqqadum airfield to determine the location of the AAA which had threatened the formation. The pilot visually acquired the AAA emplacements, but they were well dispersed in possible civilian areas, making suppression or destruction impossible without causing collateral damage. The Strike Eagles left for the tanker to take on fuel. While on the tanker, the airborne commander tasked 'Gundog' with another immediate CAOC-directed mission – this time to locate, identify and destroy a fleet of helicopters thought to be carrying WMD.

The coordinates pinpointed the targets in northern Baghdad, and accepting a higher risk due to the CAOC-directed potential WMD threat, the Strike Eagles flew through the heart of Baghdad's air defences and made three reconnaissance passes through continuous AAA and several unguided SAM launches. With no helicopters in sight, the jets departed to the west and left the Super MEZ without further incident.

Before returning for the night, 'Gundog 57' located possible Scud missile launchers in south-west Baghdad and radioed the coordinates to the airborne commander. He confirmed it was a probable SSM storage site and cleared 'Gundog' to engage any military targets. The two F-15Es once again utilised a night buddy guide tactic, designating and destroying an SSM transporter with a GBU-12. Several other SSMs were identified in the area, as well as associated hardware, but the secondary explosions from the first attack were so considerable that subsequent strikes could not be accomplished before the flight reached minimum fuel limits.

After the third aerial refuelling, 'Gundog 58' reported an unknown vibration in his aircraft. The pilot directed a return to base and recovery of the two aircraft. Following an in-flight visual check, it was determined that there was no major damage, and no sign of any could be found by troubleshooting the numerous possible sources of airframe vibration from within the cockpit. Due to the limitations of visual checks at night using NVGs, the precise source of 'Gundog 58's' vibration was unknown. Post-flight inspection found a connector on an external fuel tank on the point of failure. A dislocated fuel tank could have caused catastrophic structural failure, posing an extreme danger to the crew.

Each jet had made three aerial refuellings during the 5.9-hour day/night mission. The flight was credited with destroying one Scud SSM and a probable second, with significant damage to the associated military hardware.

PALACE RAID

Along with anti-TBM sorties, attacks on the Iraqi leadership were

An inert 2000-lb GBU-10 with its guidance kit. The GBU-10 and -12 proved remarkably effective during OIF. Rumours circulating within the USAF several years earlier suggested that these weapons were all to be converted to JDAMs because there was no place for them on the modern battlefield. Clearly there was (*author/FJ Photography.com*)

deemed to be the war's most important missions. The airborne commander could call upon any asset to be tasked to strike suspected targets falling within this group, and the author understands that Strike Eagles flew patrols along the Syrian border in support of SF operations to detect and intercept Iraqi leaders fleeing to Syria. These missions involved much pod reconnaissance, often requiring the F-15E crew to drop to lower altitude to identify vehicles passing between the two countries.

Such was the proximity of these patrols to the border that an F-15E is reported to have come under fire from a MANPAD while conducting a low-altitude reconnaissance. It is probable the missile was fired from Syria, although there is no substantial evidence available in the public domain to corroborate this.

In addition to the pre-planned patrols and the airborne re-tasking of assets to hit TCTs, the Strike Eagle squadrons also supplied aircraft to the quick reaction AGM alert pool. QRA involved a pair of aircraft, armed with AGM-130s, being ready to take-off at short notice to strike leadership targets. On the evening of 27 March, a call came in from the CAOC to rapidly rearm the AGM alert Strike Eagles with GBU-10s so that two presidential palaces in the centre of Baghdad could be struck. Saddam Hussein or his sons were believed to be hiding there, and early strikes were essential.

The mission fell to the 336th FS, and as the armourers swarmed over the jets to replace the huge AGM-130s with GBU-10s, the four aircrew involved hastily planned the mission. The sortie was executed with precision and both targets were successfully hit. Video footage of this strike was shown during the 29 March Department of Defense press briefing.

'SALTY' AND 'BOOT'

It was while flying a KI mission north of Tikrit on 7 April – possibly in support of SF soldiers – that the conflict's only F-15E loss occurred. Capt Eric 'Boot' Das (pilot) and Maj William 'Salty' Watkins (WSO) were dropping ordnance on a target when their aircraft hit the ground.

Capt Burbach had been operating in the crash area as part of a two-ship immediately before the Das/Watkins formation relieved them. He had been re-tasked to the area from a KI sortie to strike a Roland SAM site which had been reported in the vicinity. Entering the kill box, Burbach and his front-seater were immediately fired upon by AAA. He recalled;

'We saw the flashes right off the nose, and I used the IR marker in the Litening II pod to mark their positions. We saw some convoys, but the only other thing we could see was Tikrit all lit up. Out to the west it was just like a black hole – you couldn't see anything. The weather was also bad, so we had to descend to under 12,000 ft in order to get below it. We ran some attacks from the north-east, hooking out to the west and back around again. We handed off the area to them (Das' flight) and talked them through where we'd seen – the AAA and convoys. When we landed back at base, we knew immediately that something had happened. The top three (wing leadership) were really on edge.'

Capt Meziere was due in the area immediately after Das and Watkins;

'I woke up at 0300 hrs and was flying that morning. I was walking out of my tent when someone told me that we had lost a jet. I asked who it was, and was told. I was also informed that, "We have radio contact and a

Capts Nikki Das and Eric Das at Al Udeid AB, Qatar (*Nikki Das via author*)

beacon signal from 'Salty'". I thought, "Thank God they're okay". When I got to the squadron the CO pulled everyone together and said, "That's not what's happened. We don't have contact with them. Keep your mouths shut – no e-mails, no calls, nothing".'

The rumour about the radio contact had been fuelled by the suggestion from higher headquarters that a data burst had been received from Watkins' survival radio. In fact it didn't transmit at all. Meziere again;

'We ended up flying our mission right into the same area that the jet has gone down it. It was about 0600 hrs, and we held off dropping on our targets for about 45-minutes because it felt so uncomfortable to do that when these guys might still have been down there. I called AWACS and said, "Are you sure I can drop here?" I had my wingman monitor the Guard frequency just in case either of them tried to call us, but I think that with hindsight I knew then that those guys were not going to call.'

The two 335th FS lines – 'Borax 56' and '57' – had taken off just before midnight, with the lead jet flown by 'Panzer' and No 2 by 'Boot'. Das had eaten dinner that evening with his wife, Capt Nikki Das, who was the 'Rocketeer's' intelligence officer. She remembers;

'He came over to our squadron after we'd completed our mass briefing. He wasn't actually scheduled to fly that night, but once he'd returned to the 'Chiefs' he called me to tell me that he'd fallen into a flight. Eric saw me right before he stepped (went to the jet). I asked him what he was doing, where he was going and what his call-sign was. I also made sure he had his survival radio, his blood chit and had done all that intel stuff. He gave me a kiss, we said our goodbyes and he walked away. Before I went home I asked my troops to keep an eye on the "Borax" call-sign, and asked them to wake me if there was a problem. I'd never done that before.

'At about midnight I went to bed and fell asleep at about 0250L. The crash occurred at around 0300L. And that's how they knew. My Boss saw the "Borax" call-sign come up as the lost jet and came in and woke me. I went to "ops town" and immediately called Eric's family. I had promised them that they would know if things went wrong before it ever got on CNN. I promised that I'd call them.'

'Panzer' and 'Boot' had taken over from Capt Burbach's flight, and they initially worked the kill box before being re-tasked to 'another target'. 'Panzer' reportedly saw Das release his third bomb of the evening. It impacted the target area, but was quickly followed by a second explosion as the F-15E came down. A combat search and rescue (CSAR) mission was launched, but it was recalled later that morning for unspecified reasons. The 4th FW waited for news.

It took SF troops six days to reach the site, by which time at least one Iraqi search party had already been there. The troops came under such intense fire that they had less than ten minutes to collect what

USAF Chief of Staff Gen John P Jumper salutes the US flag as it is unfolded during the internment of Maj Watkins and Capt Das at Arlington Military Cemetery in May 2003 (*USAF*)

could be found of Das and Watkins, but they were only able to find traces of 'Boot'. Nikki Das finally left the operations room and flew home the same day. She said ;

'I waited six days after the crash and left on Palm Sunday to go to Texas to be with Eric's family and wait for a definite answer. Our vigil ended on Day 11 (17 April). Mel Watkins and her family didn't find out until Saturday 19 April (the night before Easter) that "Salty" had been killed.'

It would be another month before the crash site was properly secured and Watkins' remains could be recovered. Neither man had attempted to eject, and those who saw the crash site later told the author that what remained of the jet amounted to little more than a mass of small pieces. A squadron coin carried by Watkins that night was also discovered. The 'round metal object' (RMO) – as it is known colloquially – was found burned and distorted. It was one of two such RMOs which had been taped inside a US flag and then alternately carried by crews as they flew combat missions over Iraq. Back at Al Udeid, they would sign and date a small book, effectively chronicling the life of each RMO/flag combination. That night it had been 'Salty's' turn to carry it. It is understood that the recovered RMO and its 'journal' note book were presented to 'Salty's' family.

At about the time of the second trip to the crash site an Iraqi tipped off US intelligence officials that looters had plundered the site before the first SF team had arrived the previous month. 'The enemy had been to the crash site and taken some of the remains', Nikki confirmed. The remains had been taken in an attempt to extract a fee for killing two Coalition airmen, probably without success. The two aviators' remains were found in a shallow grave in Kirkuk and were then returned to the US for DNA analysis and testing. The men were separated and buried with full military honours in May 2003. A third and final clean-up operation at the crash site was then concluded by the US Army, in which more of 'Salty' and 'Boot's' remains were recovered. The men are now buried together in the Arlington military cemetery.

But what was the cause of their demise? Enemy fire cannot be ruled out, neither can the possibility that Das – who was flying on NVGs below a low overcast – became spatially disoriented. Nikki Das concluded;

'The fact of the matter is that I'm not going to know this side of Eternity what happened that night. I knew Eric's capabilities. I knew what frame of mind he was in, and that he was not reckless. I also know that spatial disorientation can happen to anyone. There were threats in the area that night that could have taken down that aircraft – it was a high threat area – but it was impossible to put all the pieces (of wreckage) back together to try and see what happened. I'm thankful that it has been recorded as a combat loss, and that Air Force officials didn't try and

Most USAF fast jet squadrons carried American flags into combat, these being discreetly folded away into a corner of the cockpit prior to take-off. A squadron coin or two would often be taped inside the flag, and the flag/coin combination handed over to an outgoing crew upon the jet's return from a combat mission. This particular flag has been temporarily placed on the cockpit instrument coaming of an F-15C by its pilot, who is in the process of conducting his pre-flight checks (*USAF*)

The rarely seen *Steel Eagle* pods (*author/FJ Photography.com*)

SUU-20 and BDU-33 blue bomblets fitted to an F-15E. This training combination was seriously considered for use in both the CAS and urban CAS role in OIF (*author/FJ Photography.com*)

guess what happened without an investigation.'

Capt Eric Das and Maj William Watkins were both posthumously awarded the Distinguished Flying Cross and Purple Heart. They were among those crews plucked from the 333rd FS 'Lancers' specifically for the war. Watkins' wife, Maj Melissa Watkins, was also an intelligence officer attached to wing intelligence. She was at home pregnant with their second child at the time of 'Salty's' loss. There is a 'Salty' Watkins website: www.mind-spring.com/-salted1/

STEEL EAGLE

Steel Eagle was one of the more interesting projects to come out of the CAOC during the war. Once a classified 'black' project born out of the weapons research laboratories at Eglin AFB, *Steel Eagle* was a slender pod which housed acoustic sensors programmed to identify the noise signature of a Scud launcher as it passed nearby. The author understands that the device – of which only 35 were manufactured – had to be placed close to the vehicle's anticipated route of travel (within 100 ft), and it would transmit a radio signal when a match was noted.

The operational concept behind the system was somewhat similar to the Vietnam War-era project *Igloo White*, but it was fatally flawed because the Strike Eagle's weapons computer had no ballistics data to predict an accurate trajectory for the pod. Aircrew were given specific instructions on the altitude, attitude and airspeed at which to release the sensor, but it would have been almost impossible for them to have placed the pod with the necessary precision.

It is understood that of the 35 made, two pods were successfully dropped in tests at Nellis AFB by the 422nd TES, but the data derived from these drops merely validated the release characteristics of the sensor, and allowed it to be cleared for operational deployment. Accordingly, no *Steel Eagles* were dropped during OIF.

The programme is no longer classified, and at the time of writing it was uncertain whether or not the pod would be developed further. The author has learned that some consideration was given to using it in Afghanistan in 2002.

URBAN CAS

For much of the war, KI, CAS and SCAR were the F-15E's primary roles. This started to change as the enemy lost the will to fight in the open and began to retreat into urban areas for a guerrilla-style campaign. For those planning the war at squadron, wing and COAC levels, this had always been the tactic that concerned them most. It had been established before execution of OPLAN 1003V that JDAM would be the weapon of choice for precise strikes on urban targets, not only because of the accuracy of its GPS-guided weapon, but also because it offered a 500-lb warhead which could be released late to confer a near vertical impact. This was ideal for instances where a built-up area might impede the progress of a GBU-12 as it made its way to the target in a more traditional parabolic trajectory.

It was, therefore, something of a relief that the urban CAS scenario never fully materialised. Had it done so, the Strike Eagle community was prepared to employ inert concrete training bombs, and there were even plans to ship in the small BDU-33 training rounds used by students to simulate the Mk 82 500-lb dumb bomb. These small bombs, which only carry a marking charge, would have been used to highlight targets for other CAS airframes such as the A-10 Thunderbolt II.

AIRFIELD ATTACKS

During SCAR sorties over enemy airfields, the 'Chiefs' and the 'Rocketeers' both made the most of opportunities to strike Iraqi aircraft on the ground. It is estimated that the 336th FS alone destroyed over 65 fighters (mostly MiG-21s), Su-22s, MiG-23s and Su-25s. The 335th FS destroyed most of their enemy aircraft in a small number of sorties, returning with evidence of the destruction of Tu-16 'Badger', Tu-22 'Blinder', Il-76 and An-12 aircraft. Video footage of these aircraft being hit by GBU-12s suggests that some were in a state of readiness. The author has also seen pod tapes showing missiles cooking off and flying wildly away from MiG-23s and Su-22s as they are struck. In others, ejection seats can be seen firing as aircraft explode.

The Strike Eagle community was briefed before OIF that the Iraqis were dismantling and burying some

A mixed formation photograph of the various aircraft that flew from Al Udeid during OIF. The USAF fast jets, all controlled by the 379th AEW, include 4th FW F-15Es, an F-117 from the 8th FS and F-16CJs from the 22nd and 157th FSs (the latter unit being a part of the South Carolina Air National Guard). An RAF Tornado GR 4 from No 12 Sqn and an RAAF F/A-18A from No 75 Sqn complete the fast jet line up. Leading the formation is a USAF KC-135R, representing the five air refuelling units (three KC-135Rs and two KC-10As) based at Al Udeid during OIF (*USAF*)

An F-117 leads a trio of 336th FS F-Strike Eagles towards the runway at Al Udeid in late April 2003. Note the Tornados, Hornets and Fighting Falcons parked to the right of the taxiway (*USAF*)

of their aircraft. This became a source of amusement and bafflement, but it is not clear whether any attempt was made to target these burial sites.

The Iraqis had few surprises for the Coalition. They did, however, try to employ countermeasures, sometimes to good effect. There were at least five main GPS jamming sites in and around Baghdad which remained active for much of the war. Despite two being struck with precision munitions (GPS weapons, no less), the effectiveness of their jamming output was enough to disrupt the flow of operations. In some instances the jamming degraded GPS guidance enough to prevent GPS weapons being dropped because accuracy would have fallen outside the ROE. In others, GPS jamming was sufficiently severe to force F-15Es to revert to traditional INS. This was not a severe hindrance, as peacetime training had placed an emphasis on getting the job done without GPS, but it did come as a surprise to many. This was the first real war to test the vulnerability of GPS-dependent systems.

While it would be disingenuous to suggest that the war was significantly hindered by GPS jamming, it is still possible to claim that critics had been wrong to state that such anti-GPS systems would only have a limited application in modern warfare. In particular, it was suggested that GPS jammers could only be effective along a very narrow corridor. That hypothesis turned out to be inaccurate.

DCA AND ESCORT

Because of the non-existent air threat posed by the IrAF, the F-15Cs returned home early, leaving the Australian F/A-18s of No 75 Sqn and

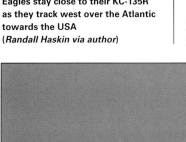

On the way home, a gaggle of Strike Eagles stay close to their KC-135R as they track west over the Atlantic towards the USA (*Randall Haskin via author*)

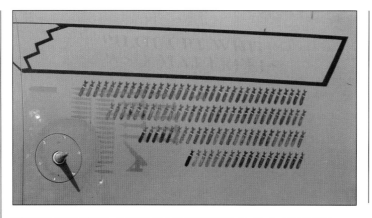

A rare shot of 'Chief's' jet 89-0483, its new mission tally having been applied directly over the faded old ones that denote its previous service over Afghanistan during OEF in 2002. Proof, if it was needed, that the 335th FS has been in the thick of things (*Greg Craven via author*)

Seen back at Seymour Johnson in the summer of 2003, this jet has had its nose art removed as per a wing directive, but its bomb tally has been allowed to remain, for the time being at least (*author/FJ Photography.com*)

4th FW F-15Es at Al Udeid to perform DCA and escort missions. The Australians had initially flown just DCA in the early days of OIF, but had soon switched to the CAS mission when the potential threat posed by the IrAF failed to materialise. The 'Rocketeers' and 'Chiefs' had also flown numerous DCA sorties from the beginning of the war, although these flights invariably ended in a little SCAR once the vulnerability time for their charges was up. Despite being configured for aerial combat, these jets had also sortied with two GBU-12s on their bomb racks, so on leaving the CAP station they could enter a nearby kill box, find two targets and then 'drop iron'. It was an interesting use of the F-15E's dual role capability, although perhaps not an approach suited to fighting a more potent adversary.

As OIF moved towards its end in late April, Gen Tommy Franks, Commander US Central Command, toured several Coalition units inside Iraq. He flew aboard an SF C-130 transport and landed at remote strips to meet the troops. It was the 'Rocketeers' who were chosen to provide Franks' fighter escort, and it was a responsibility the unit relished.

The 4th FW redeployed home from mid-April onwards, routing once again via Moron AB, in Spain. The wing received a rapturous welcome once back in North Carolina.

LOOKING TO THE FUTURE

During OIF, the Strike Eagle once again proved to be the mainstay of US military airpower. The 4th FW left Iraq having learned some hard lessons, but its overall contribution is irrefutable and uncontested. Without it, the politicians would have been unable to impose regime change and the CAOC itself would have been severely hampered in its ability to wage the fluid and dynamic war that was OIF. As in previous conflicts, the F-15E went where no other aircraft could go, and did so around the clock. To their credit, the 'Chiefs' and 'Rocketeers' 'surged' at the peak of the conflict for 11 straight days, flying as many as 96 sorties a day.

The 336th FS recorded a total time of 5937.9 hours flown during the operation, 4788.7 of which were accumulated during 1768 individual combat sorties. The F-15E finished the war with a mission capable rate of 84.1 per cent – higher than any other USAF fighter apart from the F-117.

With the conflict over, the Strike Eagle community now had to evaluate its future training programme, and consider the tactics to be employed in the next non-traditional war. Afghanistan had set that ball rolling and Iraq gave it added momentum. Within months of its end there was an official USAF evaluation of the feasibility of operating the F-15E in the FAC(A) role. There was also enthusiasm among crews at Seymour Johnson for the formation of an official F-15E FAC(A) school.

As a result of the hugely successful SCAR missions flown by the 4th FW in OIF, Strike Eagle pilots and WSOs should expect to find themselves being officially schooled and accredited in order to conduct FAC(A) sorties in future conflicts (*author/FJ Photography.com*)

SNIPER AND LITENING II

Perhaps the hottest topic of conversation within the Strike Eagle ranks was the replacement pod for the LANTIRN AAQ-14. The Litening II certainly had its place, and added some capabilities to Strike Eagle operations in the desert, but it fell short of the expectations of the next wave of F-15E aviators to be involved in combat operations. The alternative to Litening II is the Lockheed Martin Sniper Extended Range pod, which is currently being tested but is not yet ready for operational deployment.

Sniper (an Advanced Targeting Pod) is expected to be up to ten times more accurate than the LANTIRN, with triple its recognition range and twice the resolution. It is also able to acquire targets at altitudes of up to 50,000 ft – double that of the LANTIRN pod. Sniper XR has been designed for current and future fighter aircraft. Incorporating a high-resolution, mid-wave third generation FLIR, a dual-mode laser and a CCD-TV, along with a laser spot tracker and a laser marker, Sniper is expected to improve target detection/identification capabilities. 'Rocketeers' Instructor WSO Capt Joe Siberski commented;

'I'm told that when we get Sniper, we'll be able to obtain JDAM-quality coordinates. I'm also told you don't have to depend on the EO camera on Sniper like we did for Litening. Supposedly, the Sniper IR picture compensates for blooming, fires, etc., and works like a champ. How much fun would it be to have a Strike Eagle – which can defend itself at medium altitude – passing coordinates to a data link-equipped bomber with a "bazillion" JDAMS? While the bomber takes care of the fixed targets, the "Strikes" (F-15Es) can get the movers with LGBs. I dare to dream. That pretty much says it all. That's the main reason we want a better pod, and Litening was sitting on the shelf when OIF kicked off. Now that its over, the 'Guard can have their pods back and we'll take Sniper.'

DATA LINKS

The Strike Eagle's lethality over Iraq was certainly enhanced by the ZSW-1 IDLP and AAQ-14 DLP, but its seems that their potential had not been fully realised. Both pods were essential for AGM missions, and they were also used to receive Predator UAV uplinks as TCT targets became available, but these instances were few and far between. And there was a catch. *Gold Pan* (a data link system used to receive and transmit imagery and data from ground-based transmitting stations) required dedicated ground support vehicles to beam imagery up to the waiting aircraft. In OIF, the *Gold Pan* RTPS relay van was based in Kuwait, and not positioned near the frontline where it may have proved useful. The net result was that whenever an F-15E crew wanted to get the 'predator pay-per-view', it had to fly south and orbit down near the border area where Kuwait, Saudi Arabia and Iraq meet to come within range of the RTPS van's transmissions. According to Capt Haskin;

'We only really used the pods during OSW, and even then it was still a sort of proof-of-concept thing. Once OIF kicked off, there were simply so many targets out there anyway that there was no need to even use the *Gold Pan* system. I never personally got actual target updates from it.'

With a very limited application on the battlefield due to the range issues associated with *Gold Pan* van transmissions, it was not surprising that FDL was rapidly superseding *Gold Pan*. The reality was that FDL was a much better means of rapidly passing target information to the Strike Eagle anywhere on the battlefield. The CAOC could get target information to the crew via JSTARS or Global Hawk, and had no need to pass data to the RTPS van for it to be retransmitted to the F-15Es as they entered the holding pattern.

The beauty of FDL was that it kept things simple and straightforward. A WSO could call up another WSO and tell him to 'hook his des' to help sort the targets on the

The FDL data link was likely to render Gold Pan obsolete. At the time of writing, it currently allows data sharing between C3I and reconnaissance assets such as this E-3 AWACS, but future improvements could mean that live video feeds from UAVs such as Predator and Global Hawk will be permitted too (*USAF*)

ground. AWACS or JSTARS could send the F-15E a new target track right then and there. All the WSO had to do was look at his SIT display, hook the new track with his acquisition cursors and tell the pilot that the new steering was up on the HUD.

Despite Seymour Johnson wing leadership insistence that *Gold Pan* was being developed in a more focused manner, it seemed obvious that the F-15E aircrew involved in Iraq saw the future in the development of Link-16 and the FDL terminal in the aircraft instead. Immediately after the war there were bandwidth considerations to address, but it was, apparently, entirely feasible to structure the FDL network in such as way as to allow live video feed to be transmitted over the network. If such a capability can be integrated into FDL, then the future of *Gold Pan* seems to be in question. The pods themselves would remain essential for AGM missions, but would they be used for anything else? Only time will tell.

STICKING TO THE BASICS

The core focus of the training for new Strike Eagle pilots and WSOs at the FTU at Seymour seems unlikely to change. The Strike Eagle was built with interdiction and deep-strike in mind, and the core competencies necessary to get these jobs done lend themselves well to the emerging tactics and profiles flown in the previous two years by the F-15E. Some crews might wish that they could be free of the nuclear strike role in the future, for removing from operational crews the time-consuming burden of staying current in this role would permit them to hone their KI/CAS, SCAR and, possibly, FAC(A) skills to an even finer point.

At the time of writing the F-15E was at last receiving JDAM. Indeed, the first F-15E squadron to receive it (494th FS/48th FW) was expected to declare JDAM Initial Operating Capability early in 2004. With JDAM onboard, the Strike Eagle surely represents the most potent, utilitarian, multi-role fighter anywhere in the world. What's more, the Strike Eagle will be able to employ JDAM with greater ease, effectiveness and creativeness than any other JDAM dropper currently in operational service.

In early 2004 it seems that with a two-man crew, powerful air-to-ground radar, LANTIRN/AAQ-28 and superb all-weather capabilities, the F-15E is going to take some beating.

JDAM has finally arrived in the F-15E world, its addition to the Strike Eagle's burgeoning arsenal being seen as the icing on the cake. This photographs shows five inert GBU-31 JDAMs being released from the 412th Test Wing's F-15E 87-0180 during a proving flight from Edwards AFB (*USAF*)

APPENDICES

EXAMPLE OF AN OPERATION *IRAQI FREEDOM* AIR TASKING ORDER

Written in abbreviated code, this Air Tasking Order (ATO) contains all the information relating to a typical strike mission package as flown during Operation *Iraqi Freedom*. This particular ATO is from an F-15E Fighter Training Unit B-course training mission

TASKUNIT / 23 WG POPE AFB NC
(Unit tasked: 23rd Wing, Pope AFB, North Carolina)

MSNDAT / A9641 / A / HOG 21 / 4XA10 /CAS / 0166 / A/R / B/A / MK- 82 //
(Mission Data, mission number, call-sign, aircraft type and quantity, weapon type)

MSNLOC / __1010L / __1110L / DARKSTAR / 278.2 / 293.5 //
(Mission data, times and frequencies)

TGT LOC / __1020 / __1040 / / NVD / N3546W07552/ AAA / ARTILLERY //
(Target location, steer point times, coordinates and target type)

CONTROL / E-3 / BANDSAW / 278.2 / 293.5 / BROADCAST CONTROL, BULLSEYE
FORMAT //
(Command & Control data, aircraft type, call sign, frequencies and broadcast control type, with the choices being either Bulls-eye or BRAA format).

The rest of the ATO takes the same flow, but details other mission assets. In this case it includes two 1st FW F-15Cs, call-sign 'Exxon 11' and 'Exxon 12', providing OCA; and an EA-6B from MAG 14, call-sign 'Zapper 14', providing SEAD support.

AMPN / CLEAR TEXT / NOTIONAL, PACKAGE FLOW IS PER EAGLE 01 //

TASKUNIT / 1 FW LANGLEY AFB VA

MSNDAT / A8621 / A / EXXON 11 / 2XF15C / OCA / 0144 / A/R / BA/ BA //

MSNLOC / __1010L / __1110L / DARKSTAR / 278.2 / 293.5 //

TGT LOC / __1012 / __1040 / AIR THREAT AS REQD / AS REQD / //

CONTROL / E-3 / BANDSAW / 278.2 / 293.5 / TACTICAL CONTROL, BULLSEYE

FORMAT //

AMPN / CLEAR TEXT / NOTIONAL, INGRESS FLOW AND FORWARD CAP LOCATION IS PER EAGLE 01 //

TASKUNIT / MAG 14 / CHERRY POINT MCAS NC

MSNDAT / A5612 / A / ZAPPER 14 / 1XEA-6B / SEAD / 0131 / A/R / N/A / N/A //

MSNLOC / __1010 / __1110 / BARNYARD / 278.2 / 293.5 //

TGT LOC / __1015 / __1035 / AS REQD / AS REQD / AS REQD / FLOW IS AS PER EAGLE

01 DIRECTION //

CONTROL / E-3 / BANDSAW / 278.2 / 293.5 / BROADCAST ONLY , BULLSEYE

FORMAT //

AMPN / CLEAR TEXT // NOTIONAL, HARM and JAM //

OPERATION *IRAQI FREEDOM* F-15 EAGLE SERIALS

F-15E (compiled by Steve Huckvale)

335th FS/4th FW

Serial	Nose art/remarks
87-0186	marked as 4th FW CO's aircraft (crashed 4/6/03 in US)
87-0196	
87-0199	
88-1670	
88-1674	
88-1676	
88-1683	(no name - Grim Reaper head and playing cards artwork)
88-1686	*POW MIA You Are Not Forgotten*
88-1694	OIF loss on 7/4/03
88-1695	
Serial	Nose art/remarks
88-1696	
88-1701	
88-1708	

Serial	Nose art/remarks
89-0471	
89-0472	
89-0476	*GREAT DEATH*
89-0478	
89-0483	US, UK and Australian flags over map of Iraq
89-0484	*CRAZY 8's*
89-0486	*CREW DAWGS*
89-0487	*"Lucky"* (marked as 335th FS CO's aircraft)
89-0493	*493 NUMBER OF THE BEAST*
89-0496	
89-0498	*Morbid Angel* on canopy rail
89-0502	
90-0229	
90-0230	*NANCY MARY*
90-0232	

336th FS/4th FW

Serial	Nose art/remarks
87-0181	Lady Katherine (also marked as 4th OG CO's aircraft)
87-0195	4-WARNED
88-1668	"THE BIRD OF PREY"
88-1669	
88-1671	Shangri-La II
88-1672	(no name - Dragon and Scales of Justice artwork)
88-1673	SOUTHERN COMFORT
88-1675	SNEAKY CARROT
88-1682	MIGHTY MOUSE
88-1687	BACK FOR MORE MAD DUCK IV
88-1688	
88-1690	DARKNESS FALLS
88-1700	DRAGON BETTY II
88-1706	THE SADDAM HUNTER
89-0474	A CRY FOR THE FALLEN
89-0485	Memphis Belle III
89-0488	ROCKET EXPRESS
89-0490	SOUTHERN OUTLAW
89-0492	WHAT GOES AROUND COMES AROUND
89-0494	"Dirty Bird"
89-0495	BOMBAY 'SAPPHIRE' SHAKEN . . . NOT STIRRED
89-0501	Lokita's Wrath
89-0503	Taz (also marked as 336th FS CO's aircraft)
89-0505	Hoosier Daddy
90-0231	CAPTAIN AMERICA

F-15C

71st FS/1st FW (unconfirmed)

Serial

80-0038
81-0022
81-0025
81-0026
81-0029
81-0038
81-0042
82-0009
82-0011
82-0012
82-0014
82-0016
82-0019
82-0036
82-0038
83-0012
83-0013
83-0017
83-0025
83-0047
83-0048

94th FS/1st FW (unconfirmed)

78-0514
78-0525
78-0548
80-0004

80-0029
81-0020
81-0031
81-0032
81-0033
81-0037
81-0039
81-0040
81-0041
81-0050
82-0024
82-0025
82-0037
83-0010
83-0011
83-0014
83-0023
83-0024
83-0036
83-0046
84-0008

67th FS/18th FW

78-0474 (borrowed from 44th FS/18th FW)
78-0485
78-0491
78-0500
78-0545 (borrowed from 44th FS/18th FW)

58th FS/33rd FW

78-0490
78-0549
79-0053
79-0065
79-0066
79-0075
79-0078
80-0002
80-0011
81-0021
81-0054
82-0029
85-0102

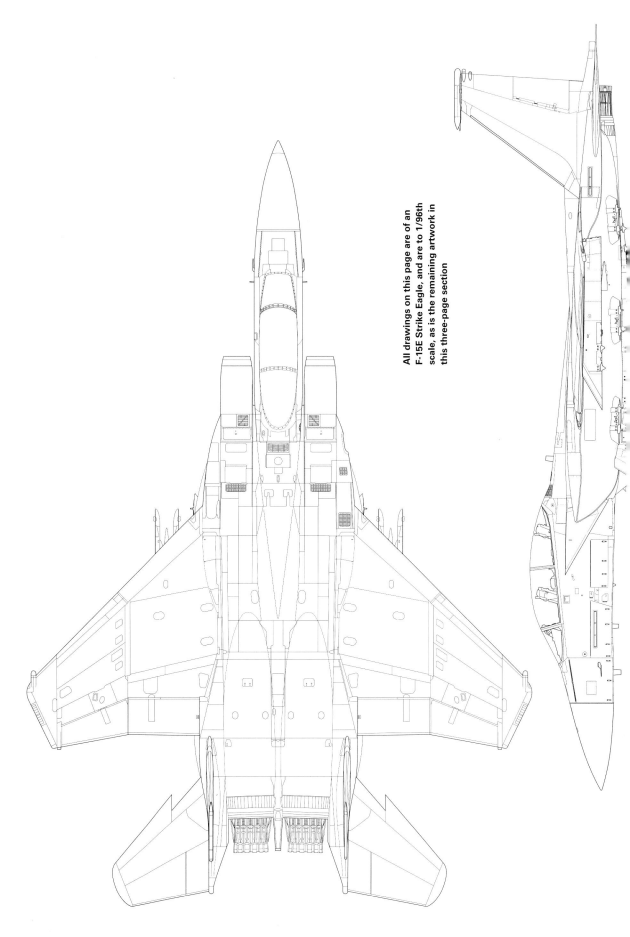

All drawings on this page are of an F-15E Strike Eagle, and are to 1/96th scale, as is the remaining artwork in this three-page section

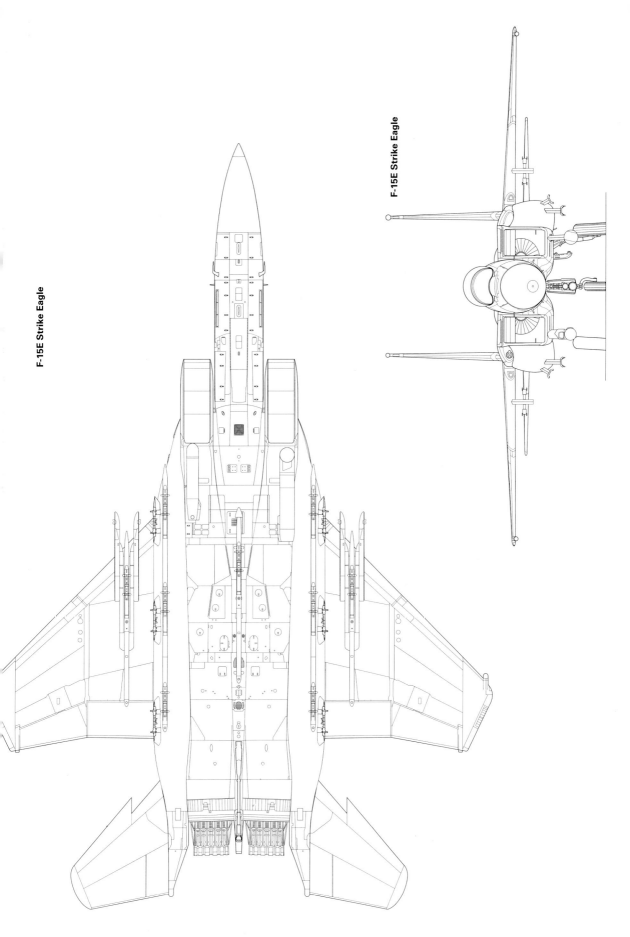

F-15E Strike Eagle

F-15E Strike Eagle

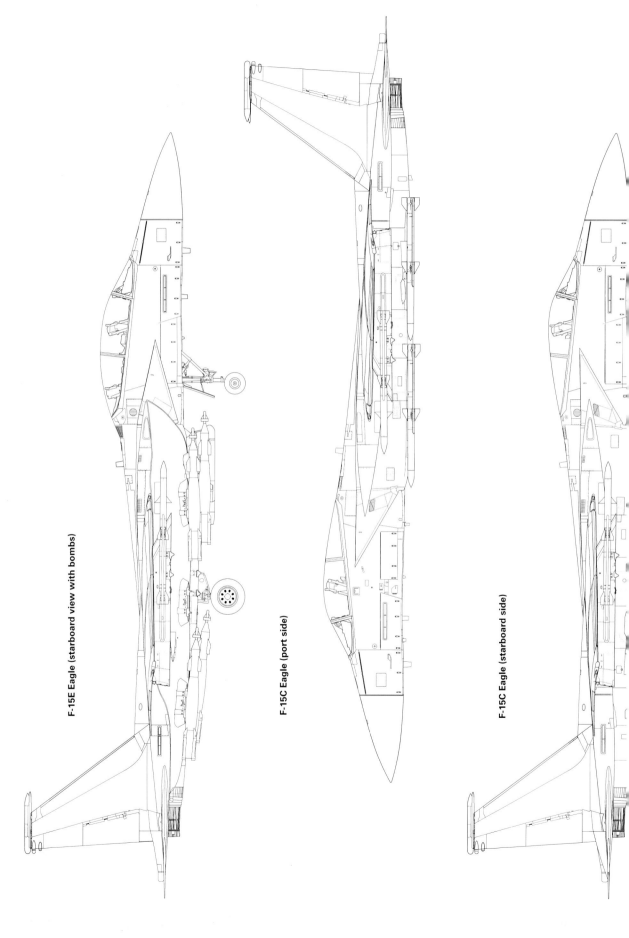

F-15E Eagle (starboard view with bombs)

F-15C Eagle (port side)

F-15C Eagle (starboard side)

COLOUR PLATES

1
F-15E AF 89-0485 of the 336th FS/4th FW, Al Udeid AB, Qatar, March-April 2003
Adorned with *Memphis Belle III* nose art (applied by Airman 1st Class Michael Hamm of the 336th FS), this aircraft was one of only a handful of F-15Es to drop a GBU-10C LGB during OIF. Other mission markings applied to this aircraft indicate that in addition to LGBs, it also dropped unguided Mk 82 500-lb bombs on three missions. 89-0485 has been a part of the 4th TFW/FW since its delivery from McDonnell Douglas' St Louis plant on 26 October 1990, and in that time the Strike Eagle has served with the wing's 334th and 335th FSs, prior to being transferred to the 336th FS in October 1997. A Block 47 airframe, 89-0485 was the 107th F-15E built. It also saw service in the 1991 Gulf War.

2
F-15E 88-1668 of the 336th FS/4th FW, Al Udeid AB, Qatar, March-April 2003
Christened *"THE BIRD OF PREY"*, this Block 45 aircraft was the 52nd Strike Eagle constructed, and was originally issued to the 335th TFS after its arrival at Seymour Johnson on 13 September 1989. Switching to the 336th TFS soon afterwards, it has remained with the 'Rocketeers' ever since. 88-1668 has seen more combat than most, having participated in Operation *Desert Storm* in 1991 and Operation *Enduring Freedom* over Afghanistan in 2001-02, before being called into action once again over Iraq in 2003. Its nose art was applied by Airman 1st Class Ryan Stafford.

3
F-15E 88-1690 of the 336th FS/4th FW, Al Udeid AB, Qatar, March-April 2003
This Strike Eagle, identified as E-74 by builder McDonnell Douglas, was the 74th F-15E to roll off the St Louis production line. Flown exclusively by the 'Rocketeers' since its arrival at Seymour Johnson on 22 December 1989, the jet was christened *DARKNESS FALLS* during OIF. It was was one of only four 336th FS jets to release an AGM-130 stand-off guided missile during the opening hours of the conflict. A Block 46 F-15E, it too participated in the 1991 Gulf War.

4
F-15E 89-0490 of the 336th FS/4th FW, Al Udeid AB, Qatar, March-April 2003
This aircraft was adorned with Warner Brothers-inspired artwork, and the name *Southern Outlaw*, by SSgt Jason Henton. A Block 48 aircraft (the 112th F-15E built) which was delivered to the 4th TFW's 334th TFS on 12 December 1990, 89-0490 was transferred to the 336th FS in April 1996. The Strike Eagle boasts a single GBU-24 Enhanced Paveway III drop amongst its tally of ordnance released during OIF.

5
F-15E 89-0505 of the 336th FS/4th FW, Al Udeid AB, Qatar, March-April 2003
A Block 48 airframe, and identified by McDonnell Douglas as F-15E E127, this jet was decorated with the scantily clad *Hoosier Daddy* by Airman Shawn Hinkle. Delivered to the 4th TFW on 30 April 1991, 89-0505 served with the 335th TFS until it moved to the 336th FS in November 1995.

6
F-15E 89-0231 of the 336th FS/4th FW, Al Udeid AB, Qatar, March-April 2003
CAPTAIN AMERICA adorns 89-0231, this artwork having been created by Airman 1st Class Ryan Stafford once more. Credited with numerous missions and GBU-12 and Mk 82 bomb drops, this Block 49 airframe was the 133rd F-15E built. Delivered to the 4th TFW on 16 August 1991, 89-0231 has served exclusively with the 'Rocketeers'.

7
F-15E 88-1682 of the 336th FS/4th FW, Al Udeid AB, Qatar, March-April 2003
A veteran of the 1991 Gulf War, 88-1682 was assigned the legendary *MIGHTY MOUSE* monicker, and painted accordingly by SSgt Jason Henton. The aircraft is shown with 14 GBU-12 mission markings, although it should be noted that all of the profiles in this volume depict the aircraft straight after they had received their nose art at Al Udeid in early April 2003 – additional bomb silhouettes were applied as the jets completed more missions. *MIGHTY MOUSE* is a Block 45 Strike Eagle, being the 66th F-15E built.

8
F-15E 89-0494 of the 336th FS/4th FW, Al Udeid AB, Qatar, March-April 2003
With 17 individual mission markings dating from March and April 2003, *"Dirty Bird"* was the fifth Block 48 Strike Eagle (and the 116th built overall) delivered to the USAF. Arriving at Seymour Johnson on 29 January 1991, the aircraft served with the 334th TFS until transferred to the 336th FS in April 1997. Airman 1st Class William Gillmer applied the artwork to this jet.

9
F-15E 88-1687 of the 336th FS/4th FW, Al Udeid AB, Qatar, March-April 2003
BACK FOR MORE MAD DUCK IV is another of SSgt Jason Henton's creations. The 71st F-15E built, this aircraft boasted two GBU-12, one Mk 82 and one GBU-10 mission markings by early April 2003. 88-1687 (a Block 45 jet), was delivered to the 4th TFW on 20 December 1989. Assigned to the 335th TFS, it saw action with the unit in Operation *Desert Storm* and was transferred to the 'Rocketeers' in July 1992.

10

F-15E 88-1706 of the 336th FS/4th FW, Al Udeid AB, Qatar, March-April 2003

Senior Airman Richard Bugbee penned the humorous caricature of Saddam Hussein onto this machine (the 90th F-15E built). Delivered to the 335th TFS on 15 June 1990, *THE SADDAM HUNTER* participated in Operation *Desert Storm*. Assigned to the 334th TFS in October 1991, 88-1706 joined the 336th FS in April 1996. This Block 46 Strike Eagle had nine GBU-12 and one Mk 82 mission markings to its credit at the time this artwork was applied at Al Udeid in early April 2003.

11

F-15E 88-1700 of the 336th FS/4th FW, Al Udeid AB, Qatar, March-April 2003

DRAGON BETTY II featured the most flamboyant artwork of all the 4th FW's F-15Es sent into combat, and once again it was created by Jason Henton. Some 19 GBU-12, 1 Mk 82, 4 GBU-10 and a single AGM-130 mission marking make for an already impressive tally at the time these markings were observed on 16 April 2003. The aircraft, a Block 46 jet (84th F-15E built), was delivered to the the 4th TFW's 335th TFS on 16 April 1990 and subsequently saw combat with the squadron during the 1991 Gulf War. Transferred to the 334th TFS 'Eagles' in April 1991, 88-1700 remained with the unit until passed on to the 336th FS in April 1996.

12

F-15E 89-0474 of the 336th FS/4th FW, Al Udeid AB, Qatar, March-April 2003

A CRY FOR THE FALLEN (artwork by SSgt Anthony Wolfe) was one of four F-15Es to drop GBU-28 'bunker-busting' LGBs over Iraq. The weapon was employed twice by the 4th FW in OIF, bombs hitting a Presidential Palace and an IADS underground bunker complex. It is not know exactly which mission this F-15E participated in, although both strikes were highly-successful. A Block 47 (96th F-15E built) machine, this jet was delivered to the 335th TFS/4th TFW on 10 August 1990. It saw combat in Operation *Desert Storm* with this unit, and was then transferred to the 334th TFS in April 1991. 89-0474 was issued to the 336th FS in March 1996.

13

F-15E 89-0495 of the 336th FS/4th FW, Al Udeid AB, Qatar, March-April 2003

Adorned with artwork applied by Strike Eagle pilot Capt Randall Haskin, 89-0495 *BOMBAY 'SAPPHIRE' . . . SHAKEN NOT STIRRED* comes complete with the recipe for a 'Zappa' Martini – Gin, Vermouth and Tritonol'! The aircraft is a Block 48 jet, being the 117th F-15E built. Delivered to the 334th TFS/4th TFW on 28 January 1991, and thus missing out on Operation *Desert Storm*, this Strike Eagle became a 'Rocketeer' as long ago as July 1992.

14

F-15E 89-0476 of the 335th FS/4th FW, Al Udeid AB, Qatar, March-April 2003

The 98th F-15E built, 89-0476 already had 42 Operation *Desert Storm* combat missions under its belt prior to playing its part in OIF. The Block 47 machine, nicknamed *GREAT DEATH*, also saw much action in OEF in 2002. Having only ever served with the 335th FS, this jet was first delivered to 4th TFW on 24 July 1990.

15

F-15E 89-0487 of the 335th FS/4th FW, Al Udeid AB, Qatar, March-April 2003

89-0487 was not only the 'Chiefs'' flagship in 2003, but it is also the sole F-15E to have scored an air-to-air kill. A veteran of the first Gulf War in 1991, *"Lucky"* scored a direct hit on a Mi-24 'Hind' helicopter gunship as it threatened US Special Forces (SF) deep inside Iraq on 14 February 1991. Capts Richard Bennett (pilot) and Dan Bakke (WSO) pickled a single GBU-10 at their hovering target some six miles away, having been called in by AWACS to support the SF troops after they had reported seeing several Iraqi helicopters off-loading troops in their immediate vicinity. Acquisition of the 'Hind' had come first from the jet's radar, but a visual tally through the AAQ-14 pod quickly followed. Neither Bennett or Bakke were sure that the bomb would hit the Mi-24, but to their relief it vapourised 30 seconds after the 2000-lb GBU-10 LGB had left their jet. The USAF did not officially recognise the kill until 2 November 2001. The 109th F-15E built (as part of Block 47), *"Lucky"* was delivered to the 335th TFS/4th TFW on 13 November 1990. Transferred to the 334th TFS in April 1991, it returned to the 'Chiefs' six months later. Switching to the 336th TFS in April 1993, 89-0487 became a 335th FS machine for a third time in May 1998. It is depicted here with almost 100 bomb markings to its credit.

16

F-15E 89-0493 of the 335th FS/4th FW, Al Udeid AB, Qatar, March-April 2003

493 NUMBER OF THE BEAST has served with the 'Chiefs' since August 1991, having initially been delivered to the 334th TFS/4th TFW on 28 January 1991. The 115th F-15E built, it was constructed by McDonnell Douglas as part of Block 58. OIF saw the 335th FS use heavily-stylised bomb markings that harked back to those used during World War 2. Recently returned from OEF, several 'Chiefs' jets had their *Enduring Freedom* mission tallies overpainted with newer OIF markings.

17

F-15E 88-1683 of the 335th FS/4th FW, Al Udeid AB, Qatar, March-April 2003

A veteran of 49 combat mission during *Desert Storm*, 88-1683 subsequently flew more bombing sorties in 2001-02 when it participated in OEF with the 'Chiefs'. The 67th F-15E built (as part of Block 45), this aircraft was delivered to the 336th TFS/4th

TFW on 13 December 1989. Having served with the 334th and 335th FSs since then, the jet stated its present spell with the 'Chiefs' in July 1996.

18

F-15E 89-0483 of the 335th FS/4th FW, Al Udeid AB, Qatar, March-April 2003

Depicted prior to its arrival at Al Udeid, this Block 47 jet (the 105th F-15E built) has been a 335th FS jet since April 1996. Delivered to the 334th TFS/4th TFW on 26 October 1990, the fighter has seen combat in *Desert Storm*, OEF and OIF.

19

F-15C 82-0019 of the 71st FS/1st FW, Incirlik (Turkey) and Sheikh Isa (Bahrain), February-April 2003

This jet was the 71st FS's flagship during the 1st FW's deployment to Turkey and then Bahrain during OIF. The unit's sister squadron, the 94th FS, spent the war on the ground at Incirlik AB, Turkey. The 71st deployed 12 F-15Cs, the last of which returned to the US on 25 April 2003. Delivered to the 27th TFS/1st TFW on 6 October 1983, this Block 33 airframe has been in the inventory of the 71st FS since May 1990. Indeed, it deployed to Dhahran AB, Saudi Arabia, with the unit as part of Operation *Desert Shield* in August 1990.

20

F-15C 85-0102 of the 58th FS/33rd FW, King Faisal AB, Saudi Arabia, February-April 2003

Painted up as the 33rd FW flagship, this Block 39 Eagle has three kills to its credit dating back to the 1991 Gulf War. The first came on 29 January 1991 when Capt David Rose scored a kill against an Iraqi MiG-23 during an OCA sortie. The second and third kills came by way of Capt Anthony Murphy, who was wingman in a section of two F-15Cs flying BARCAP along the Iraq/Iran border on 7 February 1991. He used AIM-7 Sparrows to engage and destroy a gaggle of escaping Su-7/17/22 'Fitters' in a rear-aspect tail chase. His flight lead, Col Rick Parsons (then 33rd TFW CO), downed an Su-7/17/22 with an AIM-9 moments later. This jet has served exclusively with the 33rd FW since its delivery on 15 October 1986.

21

F-15C 79-0078 of the 58th FS/33rd FW, King Faisal AB, Saudi Arabia, February-April 2003

Nicknamed the 'Gorrillas', the 58th FS deployed to the Gulf on 6 March 2003 with 13 jets and 22 pilots. Among them was this Block 26 Eagle, which was formerly a charge of the 53rd TFS/36th TFW at Bitburg AB, in Germany. The fighter (delivered to the USAF on 9 June 1981) saw combat with the 53rd from 'PSAB' during *Desert Storm*, Capt Thomas Dietz claiming two MiG-21 kills with it on 6 February 1991. 1Lt Bob Hehemann, who was Dietz's wingman that day, downed two Su-25s in the same engagement. 79-0078 arrived at the 33rd FG after seeing service with the 19th FS/3rd Wing from August 1994 through to October 1998.

Colour Nose Art Gallery

1
F-15E 88-1700 of the 336th FS/4th FW
(*All nose art photographs by Randall Haskin via author*)

2
F-15E 88-1687 of the 336th FS/4th FW

3
F-15E 88-1671 of the 336th FS/4th FW

4
F-15E 89-0476 of the 335th FS/4th FW

5
F-15E 89-0493 of the 335th FS/4th FW

6
F-15E 88-1683 of the 335th FS/4th FW

7
F-15E 88-1672 of the 336th FS/4th FW

8
F-15E 90-0231 of the 336th FS/4th FW

9
F-15E 88-1686 of the 335th FS/4th FW

10
F-15E 88-1668 of the 336th FS/4th FW

11
F-15E 89-0485 of the 336th FS/4th FW

12
F-15E 89-0474 of the 336th FS/4th FW

13
F-15E 89-1706 of the 336th FS/4th FW

14
F-15E 88-1682 of the 336th FS/4th FW

15
F-15E 88-1675 of the 336th FS/4th FW

16
F-15E 89-0494 of the 336th FS/4th FW

17
F-15E 89-0505 of the 336th FS/4th FW

18
F-15E 87-0195 of the 336th FS/4th FW

19
F-15E 89-0490 of the 336th FS/4th FW

INDEX

References to illustrations are shown in **bold**. Colour Plates are prefixed 'pl.' and Colour Nose Art Gallery plates 'na.', with page and caption locators in (brackets).